Soldier Soldier Squaddie Squaddie

Christian Franks

Clink
Street

Published by Clink Street Publishing 2021

Copyright © 2021

First edition.

ISBN:
978-1-913962-95-1 - paperback
978-1-913962-96-8 - ebook

Acknowledgements

.

Al Peasland
Geoff Thompson
Nigel Payne
Ann Evans

*To all those fine men and women who have died
and been injured whilst serving in the British
armed forces.*

*To all those fine men and women who have served
in the British armed forces.*

*To all those who have aided the fine men
and women who have served in the British
armed forces.*

*To the medical staff, councilors and families who
have spent time and help, the understanding
and patience that they have shown to the men
and women who have served in the British
armed forces.*

*To all those fine men and women who are suffering
from combat stress related illness PTSD after
serving in the British armed forces.*

Contents

CHAPTER 1   Foreword   11

CHAPTER 2   Introduction   15

CHAPTER 3   The Early Days (Sprogs)   19

CHAPTER 4   New Draft   31

CHAPTER 5   No Longer New Draft   43

CHAPTER 6   Overseas   49

CHAPTER 7   Hong Kong – My Second Home   65

CHAPTER 8   Holiday   91

CHAPTER 9   South Korea   99

CHAPTER 10   Up Above The Clouds   115

CHAPTER 11   The Wart   123

CHAPTER 12   Home Sweet Home   127

CHAPTER 13   Disasters   133

CHAPTER 14   No Longer A Squaddie?   143

THE FINAL CHAPTER   12 Years on   155

Foreword

I wrote this book over 18 years and have gone through it several times, sending some parts of to publishers without them taking it on. Then it has played with my conscience, will it upset people? God how I have changed with my view to women from my early day? Was I just a thug? Is there too much swearing? Sex? Shall I get it published or not? Yes.

Shall I get it published or not? No.

Shall I get it published or not? Yes

Friends have read this book; other authors have read this book.

I have been told it is an enjoyable book that you do not want to put down, but all who have read this know me as a person, so will it appeal to people who do not know me???

I believe like for me it will be a good read for the squaddies out there who can relate to the book, but not too sure about the general public.

A proof-reader has read the book and said she thinks it's good, but I do not explain who I am, what has made me like the why I am, why I was like this?

She says the reader would just rather like this person or hate him.

So here goes a little about the main character.

The main character in this book overall is a good person, but through life has had to deal with a lot of rejection and because of this has put a shield up personally. The rejection is from childhood up to his present life. Whilst serving with the British forces he became a member of a large family which saw a lot of laughter, fun, games and violence. He has lived on the edge of life and after leaving this large family, found it hard to readjust to civilian life and has been lucky not to have been imprisoned.

He is also lucky to be alive and within his life he has been stabbed (seven times), glassed several times, bottled a few times, knuckle-dusted, baseball-batted, shot at, been used as a football by at least six heavies and dragged around a car park with his foot trapped in a car door.

He has been told he has a hard exterior but once you can break through that he is a nice person.

He stands at just under six foot and quite stocky, has a permanent frown under his dazzling blue eyes, whilst severing in the army he had a fit, stocky body, blond hair which was short as it had to be whilst serving. Was told that he was a nice-looking young man but over the years the beer has taken its toll and has now the ageing beer belly and balding head.

The book begins from him joining the British forces, learning the life in the army from being a raw recruit to becoming and old soldier, leaving the army and finding the stress of Civilian Street and adjusting to a new life, all the way to the present day. My view and now here a friend's view.

Nigel's view

Trying to describe this person in a couple of paragraphs I am finding difficult, First impressions, that frown!

It can be said he comes across as arrogant, intimidating and bloody hard work sometimes.

He has put up many barriers as he described above, he needs to be wanted and needed, trust is a bit thing in his life, he sets high standards in that department not everybody allowed in.

I met him some years ago, when we were both playing for a local rugby club – about 30 years ago, we never really got on at first as I didn't know how to take him, again this image and barriers he puts up. Some say he's like Marmite. I disagree, once you hate Marmite you always hate Marmite, that's not him, you can if you get past the barriers and get to know the real person find a totally different character and a totally different person.

The real person is loyal, he will help you in any situation and be there for you anywhere, he will give you his trust, but this has a cost, if you don't treat him with his standard and level of trust you will lose it and may never gain his trust again. Devoted, see him round his daughter and you see the true side of him, having spent a lot of time and money to gain access to her life, a lot of other people would have given up but not him. He represented himself and came away winning access to his daughter, he wasn't going to let his daughter grow up not knowing her father.

Very driven, when he gets something in his head, he has to see it through, searching for his birth mother, it was something he had to do for himself to help him move on in his life, again his stubborn determination got him results.

He will always feed off a crowd as anybody who has been on a rugby tour with him will testify either with the club he was successful at as a first team regular for ten years or later with another local club where he became the player coach. A very accomplished rugby player and later a player-coach. Finding a new rugby home and new audience for him to entertain and he certainly did that.

He lived the doorman's life to the full, the fighting, drinking and women, every weekend was full on. Having his heart broken by a girl so again a barrier went up and thought he had to treat women in a certain way, scared to drop his guard so as not to get hurt and rejected again.

Summing him up, He served his country with distinction, travelled the world (fought with most of it as well) became a father and a devoted dad, had a very successful rugby career playing for the combined services, winning county championships over the years. Tracing his birth mother and then his father (who rejected him), running his own business, a successful rugby coaching career where he won Team of the

Year and was on the front page of the *Rugby World Magazine*. Became Moroccan boxing champion on one rugby tour, discovered he has an attraction to large Scottish ladies in Aya Napa. He now even sells things that he has bought (bit of a hoarder), he has wrote a book about his life and getting it published, so it only leaves a Mrs to come along but I'm not holding my breath on that one.

Proud to call him my best friend and my life would have been very different without him around – as you get older you rely on the stories and memories you have and can tell usually over a few drinks; I don't think I have to many stories that do not involve him, thinking back now though for two guys who don't smile a lot we certainly have smiled and laughed a lot.

Introduction

Some names have been changed to protect the innocent!

Soldier or Squaddie?

There are two sides to a soldier, work and play. Working is when you are a soldier. I was a very good soldier and enjoyed my time whilst serving with my regiment in many parts of this fine world of ours.

I was asked to go on a course to become a physical training instructor and my platoon commander even came up to me in my latter years in the army and asked me to enlist for selection for G squadron of the SAS. I thought about this for all of one second and said a big fat "NO THANKS" as both seemed to be far too physical and demanding. Therefore, I declined the offers.

Then there is play. This is when we become squaddies. When we go out and let your hair down a bit and enjoy ourselves. Beer, girls and parties, this being more up my street.

How did I come about writing this book?

I had left the army and whilst away on holiday with my mates in Cyprus, we were all sat around the swimming pool recovering from the night before, drinking beers and telling jokes and funny stories.

I would be telling my mates (Baz a big six foot two lad, loved the sun but always seemed to end up with the shits and never making every night out, I grew up with Baz and have known him all my life; Nigel was a little smaller than Baz and had ginger hair, he could never finish off his beer; and then there was Andy, smaller and older than the rest of us but more lively some of the things that I got up to whilst in the army.

Nigel then said to me you should write a book.

A friend of mine had already written books about his past.

He had been a doorman for ten years and had written several books on his experiences whilst working on the doors, so I thought why not I will give it a shot?

This book is all about us squaddies, some of the things that I got up to and some of the things that my colleagues got up to. There are many soldiers who have done far worse than I have and those who have not.

I am not going to apologise for the swearing or contents because if I did, then this would not be a true reflection on what has occurred, What I will say however is that if you decide to carry on and read this book then one thing is for sure and that is you will be glad your daughter is not with me.

I am not a thug or womaniser. I hate people who hurt the young, old and animals.

But my worst enemy is probably alcohol.

I am now 32 years old working in a secure job, I have my own home, and I'm trying to start up a small building business while doing the odd night on the doors of some pubs in our town.

And yes, I'm still single.

I will never let my mother see this book because like most mothers she thinks butter would not melt in her son's mouth.

Well, that last bit was when I started the book. It should now read…

I am now 54 years old working as freelance tutor, after owning a small successful training centre. I have my own home, No longer doing the odd night on the doors. Alcohol is still my enemy and yes, I'm still single.

Back in the 70s, 80s and 90s the forces were not held in the high respect that we are now.

Life in the forces can be very strange and you can sometimes be away from your loved ones for an exceptionally long time.

There are a lot of split marriages in the forces and a lot of the times our partners will say they do not understand us and why do we have to do this or that. What I will say is if you're away on exercise for two weeks, or on the Falklands for six months, then when you come back you need to let your hair down (some excuse, I think not).

Finally, I would like to say that the British Forces (Air, Land and Sea) are the best in the world. The training may be hard, but it has been for centuries and has and will produce in the future the best soldiers/airman/sailors in the world and this has been proven.

CHAPTER 1

The Early Days (Sprogs)

I left school in 1982, there were not many jobs around for someone like me who preferred to mess around at school rather than try to get myself a decent education. I did get some CSE's but only grade 2, 3, 4 and 5, so as you can see, I was not the brain of Britain. So, I did a few YOP (Youth Opportunity) schemes which lasted for about six months with no offer of full-time employment. So, I was then persuaded to try for the Forces by my elder brother who was already in the army. So off I went to the army careers centre and before I knew it, I was off to Sutton Coldfield for a weekend assessment. This was all new to me, but I did OK, we had physical fitness tests and then written tests in all subjects, this lasted for the two days and to my surprise I found myself standing in this very clean and smart office and there behind the desk was this very smart tall officer.

He was sitting behind a nice polished desk on a nice polished parquet wooden floor. In his smart uniform, no creases just as you would expect. There was a brass paperweight on the table, and behind the table hanging halfway up the wall was a picture of Queen Elizabeth II. The officer told me sit down, he was being very friendly and then told me that I had passed my entrance tests asked me several questions and then asked me to stand up which I did.

He looked me up and down and then said you are quite tall I'm going to offer you a post with the Coldstream Guards.

Coldstream Guards I thought to myself, aren't they the ones with those funny hats who stand outside Buckingham palace and don't smile? Yes, that's them. But I didn't fancy that, I wanted to be wearing combats and shooting guns, rolling around and all the kind of Action Man stuff. So, I had a bright idea I would say yes and then just change over when I got in. So, I said yes. The officer shook my hand and wished me the best, I think he was laughing under his breath as he knew the hard training, he was sending me off to do. He knew that this young boy would never be the same again.

So off I went, walking over the polished parquet floor minding not to scrape my shoes on it and back to the train station.

The first thing I did was to tell my dad, he was chuffed to bits that I had been offered a place in the Coldstream Guards. I think he was happier than me or it may have been he was glad to see the back of me.

All I needed to do now was go for my medical, have the cough and drop and then it would be off to the army life for me.

A Little Bit About the Coldstream Guards.

Firstly, I am as proud as anyone to have served with the Coldstream Guards and I will always be. The Coldstream Guards were formed in 1650 and were raised on the orders of Oliver Cromwell to form Colonel Monck's Regiment of foot and were part of the New Model Army.

In January 1660 (two years after Cromwell's death) General Monck marched his troops to London because of political upheavals and helped to restore peace and order, which helped in returning King Charles II to the throne. King Charles then disbanded the New Model Army but decided to keep Monck's Regiment of Foot, which later became personal guards to the sovereign.

The regiment has many battle honours on our colours including Waterloo, honours in the Second World War and in recent times, we have served in the gulf, Afghanistan and Bosnia.

The Guards (Grenadier, Coldstream, Scots, Irish and Welsh) are the top infantry regiments in the world. This has been proven. The Scots and the Welsh were the main infantry regiments sent to the Falklands and any one or all of the five guard regiments would be sent to any main conflict that Britain may be engaged in. What makes us so special is that one minute we may be in Northern Ireland, Bosnia, Falklands, Afghanistan or the Gulf, and then we return to England and will then go on guard duty outside Buckingham Palace, St James Palace, Windsor Castle or the Tower of London. We aren't just the best infantry regiment but are also the best at foot drill in the world; there is no better ceremonial occasion in the world than the 'Trooping of the Colour'.

The Coldstream Guards motto is 'Nulli Secundus' which means 'Second to None'.

That's a little bit about the Guards but there could be many books written about the Guards history and the battles and VCs.

I then joined the Coldstream Guards as a recruit and went off to Pirbright to do my six months basic training. I would be doing this with the Scots Guard recruits.

I remember arriving at the train station where we were picked up from and driven on a coach to the barracks that we would be doing our basic training and being my home for the next six months. This being Pirbright. Arriving at Pirbright we watched as lads were being marched at high speed around the camp, their instructors shouting at them, squads running some with packs and tin pots on and some not, again with instructors shouting at them. some recruits were walking, and windows opened and again shouting coming from the windows and they then increased their pace.

I could not believe it. We then had to carry our own bags to the barrack room. We were all given our own beds in a 20-man room. The room was a long cold room with a shiny polished floor, the beds small metal beds with horrible itchy blankets laid on a thin mattress with one thin pillow next to it. There was a wooden locker next to the bed and a wooden bedside cabinet. There were no pictures on the walls, which were painted in a drab cold colour blue. The room felt cold and had a high ceiling and open rafters.

We were then taken down to the stores where we were given our kit, combat trousers, jacket, jumper, long johns, PT kit, boots x3, helmet, lightweight trousers and the list went on. (I can't carry all this shit ain't anyone going to help me?) Next it was off to the barbers, I knew I wouldn't be able to keep my trendy wedge haircut but I asked the barber just to go easy as I knew that what was under your hat is yours. He then brought out these shears and I was like a lamb and within a couple of minutes I was as bold as a coot.

Back to the barrack room where we had to sew on buttons and badges and sort out our kit and put it into our lockers. No TV, no video, no Atari games console. This is going to be shit I thought.

Not much sleep the first night with 19 other lads, snoring, talking and getting to know each other.

Next day locker inspection — nobody told me that the kit needed cleaning first. Corporal Stone, our barrack roomer, inspected everyone's locker shouting at a few, pulling things out of the odd locker. My locker was the last in the room I was standing there thinking this bloke is off his trolley. Then to my surprise, he lost it, he had gone easy on the rest compared to my locker, he tipped the whole of my locker onto the floor throwing my boots across the room straight at a sweaty sock (jock). He then started ranting and raving in my face and then 'smack', he punched me straight in the chest! Well, me being a clever git, moved to the end of the bed when he was doing his Tasmanian dust devil on my locker. So, when he punched me, I had a nice soft landing on my bed. The first word that came to me was "cunt" however I decided not to open my mouth and use this. I even thought about getting back up and getting stuck in but again decided not to.

Corporal Stone was an Englishman who had joined the Irish Guards.

He was about 5ft 11in and weighed about 15 stone. A little bit overweight and had been a barrack roomer for about two years and loved himself – but then I suppose someone needed to love him.

Cpl Stone did not like me that much and gave all of us recruits a hard time until we had finished our training. He was however a big fat Irish/English bully (and that was a fact).

Training was hard but on the whole fair, and all of our instructors were very good at their job and produced some good soldiers for the future (Cpl Stone was not an instructor).

Anyone who has been at Pirbright will know the sand hill. This was a massive hill of just sand. If you had been playing up or slacking off or just for extra fitness you would be taken up to the sand hill on a beasting. Up, down, up, down, up, down, 20 press-ups, up, down, up, down (sounds like having sex) up, down, 30 press-ups, piggyback, up, down, up, down, well I was feeling a little tired if I say so. This was all done with a respirator on (I've never tried sex with one on but some of the women I have had sex with would have looked better wearing one).

There was also Heartbreak, the three sisters, and the assault course. I must admit the assault course is probably one of the best in the British army. Then there was the bayonet assault course (I am led to believe this is no longer in existence) what happened here was you were made to partner up, so everybody picked their best mate, I was with mine 'Thorn'.

Thorn came from just outside Southampton. He was a very good dresser and had all the top clothes, his hair was dark and spiked up he was about 5ft 10in and had a large chest. I stayed very good friends with Thorn throughout my time in the army.

The sergeant then told us to punch each other, so in came the Oscars, "Right Thorn I will hit you first you pretend it hurts then it's your turn." This went on for a while until we were noticed. Sgt. Iron (a Scots Guard who was a hard bloke a tough solid Glaswegian but was very fair with us recruits) then said right you two, you either kick the shit out of each other, or I will kick the shit out of you both. Well, I didn't fancy getting the shit kicked out of me by this big hard member of the MacLeod family or whatever Mac clan he belonged to.

So, the punches started getting harder and harder and then I thought fuck this and we both kicked the shit out of each other. After this we all had to stand in a line with our bleeding noses and lips next door to your ex best mate and the sarge would come around with a bucket and tell you to stick your head in this. I looked down and the bucket was full of pig's guts and blood. Oh well, bollocks to it and I shoved my head in it, after this it was fix bayonets and off I went down the course shouting my fucking head off running through shit jumping over walls through fire and then I came across a dummy (no not Cpl Stone) in with the bayonet, 'splat' it was full of pigs guts, the sergeant standing there shouting, "Come on you fucking little wimp off to the next one!" So off I went under the barbed wire over the walls through the fire and onto the next dummy. This carried on for about a quarter of a mile and then it was off on a long run back to the barracks, we did a lot of long runs some with gas masks on, some without, some with webbing on, some with packs and tin pots on. We also carried logs the size of lamp posts and carried stretchers with the biggest lad having a rest on this whilst we carried him. One thing I will say is I was as fit as fuck when my training was over. We had changing parades as well. This was just another fuck about for us all.

We would be told to turn out on parade in our combats. Then told to get changed into barrack room dress and then into number two dress, PT kit, NBC kit and so on and on, only having about two minutes between each change and always after we had just sorted out our lockers.

We would then be told we had another locker inspection in half an hour.

We did a lot of drill (marching, arms drill). We did weapon training, Nuclear biological welfare training, combat training, and first aid training. Every night was spent cleaning our kit (bulling the boots, buffing our belts, cleaning our brasses, ironing, washing, sewing) then when we finished our kit it was time for our rooms and toilets (scrubbing the loo, floors, shining the windows, waxing the floors, cleaning the copper pipe work, polishing and bumpering the floors). Then was it off to our scratchers? No it was another locker inspection and then we could go to bed. (They had it a lot easier in *Full Metal Jacket*.)

When we did our foot drill (marching), all the sayings came out, "Dig your heels in," "Get your neck in the back of your collar," "Get your arms up, shoulder length."

If we were not doing this, then it would be. "Get your arms up, you ugly git or I will rip them off and hit you with the soggy end," or "Get your neck back or I will rip your head off and shit down your neck," and there was the normal ones like, "How can you be that ugly with only one head?"

We went on exercises and weekend camp, the first weekend camp we went on we were shown how to put up bashers, how to camouflage our poncho, and lay our maggot bag out. Then camouflaging ourselves and tin pots, doing the buddy-buddy system.

At dinnertime, we were split in our sections and given our lunch, chicken, oh lovely. Not this fucking one, it was still walking around! "Right, that's your lunch. Here's what you do," said Sgt Iron as he puts the chicken between his hands twisting and pulling, then off came its head (it's true what they say about chickens he threw it to the floor, and it kept on running around and around). He then showed us how to pluck it (yes pluck it, not fuck it) gut it and then cook it. When it was my turn to turn out its lights, I was told that I had lost an arm and was starving so what was I going to do? So, like a clever git that I am I said I would stand on it and twist and pull! "No" was the answer. Well I would hold it down and chop off its head. No again. Well, I'm fucking going to have to starve I said. No you're not why not use your big fucking gob? So, I had to put it squawking head and neck between my teeth and twist and pull. I killed it plucked it and gutted it but I'm a shit cook and it was not cooked properly when we came to eat it. I did not know there was that much in the job at Kentucky Fried Chicken.

After a while, we were allowed out at weekends on the piss and now and again allowed home on leave. On the piss was either down the Naffi, or down Woking or Guildford, the last two were where Sgts Iron, Lynne and Hast (Sgt Lynne being a Scots Guard, he was one of these blokes who pissed me off, tall, dark, muscular built, handsome and as fit as fuck also as hard as fuck. He must have been the fittest bloke I have ever met; would run for miles without breaking into a sweat. he was my first section commander and was a very good instructor; Sgt Hast being from the Welsh Guards, he loved his rugby and was also a very good instructor) always seemed to go but they always ended fighting with the paras, so that's where we first went because if anyone started on us we knew that our instructors were right hard bastards and they would be on our side (nothing wrong with dreaming).

Off we went on the piss. First bar, posh bar, lovely carpet leading to a nice long bar, latest optics on the bar behind and nice-looking barmaid standing next to the older publican, looking around some regulars in the corner chatting away not paying any notice to anyone else. A loving couple sitting at a table near the window, whispering sweat nothings to each other whilst gazing into each other's eyes with lustful thoughts going on in their minds. There was about six of the local youths laughing loudly around another table and a couple of other soldiers standing around.

Then we saw the local slappers sitting in the corner, so off went me and Thorn, "Hi girls come here often?" They just looked at us and laughed and said they were waiting for someone. We tried this approach on several girls without any luck, so in the next pub. another nice pub similar to the first, so I thought I would change my chat up and I went over to these two birds and said, "Hi girls, fancy a fuck?" and got the reply, "Fuck off you dickless bastard," so I took this as no!

We went into the next pub. This one was a bit run down. The carpet had been down for donkey years, beer spilt all over it. With a strong stench coming from it, as it had never been cleaned. Smoke filled the room with the healthy punters downing their favourite ales whilst puffing away. Some playing cards, some darts and the all-day pisshead asleep in the corner.

The bar was stained with the old brass bar running around it, but it was broken in places and the foam being ripped out of most of the chairs. Empty glasses still on the torn beer mats.

Eventually we pulled two right tarts they said; "You're soldiers, aren't you?" "No!" I said. I thought how can they tell (crew cut, tie and trousers in a pub full of people in jeans and long hair). I asked if the one I was with would like a drink. She replied, "Yes I will have a vodka and coke," cheeky bitch that's two drinks. Anyway, at the end of the night, I swapped a bit of spit with her; tongue wrestled for about half an hour and let her give me a Thomas the Tank.

We said our goodbyes and off Thorn and I went onto the train and back to the barracks. On the way back there were some gobby civvies sitting there who said, "Them two are fucking squaddies." "Squaddies," I said, "I ain't no squaddie. I'm a fucking soldier so go and get fucked." This sparked a reaction and I stood up said, "Fuck off." The red mist then came. "Come on then you civvy wankers, let's go for it," I said and Thorn stood up beside me. The civvies stood up. Shit, I thought, we are outnumbered, but to my relief they just gobbed off then got off the train. Someone was lucky that night. More than likely us.

Looking back now I do feel sorry for one guy. He was a smelly git and we were ordered to give him a regimental bath. So, we filled the bath up with water, bleach, toilet cleaner, Brasso, piss and anything else we could find. We then dragged him into the toilets bollock naked and threw him in the bath. We then scrubbed him with toilet brushes and bass brooms and then let him out after his screams and crying had finished. He was always clean after that but did say he needed that lesson, and he passed his training and went on to join the battalion.

There was the odd fisticuffs between us all from time to time. This has to be expected when you're with the same group of lads, day in day out. Sergeant Iron had the best idea when he caught two of the lads arguing he made us all sit down in a circle and watched the two lads kick the shit out of each other.

I had a couple of run-ins with my fellow recruits. On one occasion I was having an argument with one of my mates. We were all sitting on our own beds cleaning our kit. I was having a slanging match with this lad. He was a Scots Guard recruit, someone in the room then started winding him up which resulted in him saying, "Come on, me and you outside."

So off we went the two of us behind this drill shed. I didn't really want to fight him as we were quite good mates, but he was being a stubborn jock and still wanted to carry on, so off we went and I just punched him a few times as I was sitting on him and tried to make him see reason. He did and we both got up shook hands and went back to the barrack room.

We walked into the room everyone turned and looked at us. One of the lads asked who had won, I replied, "No one, it was a draw," but my defeated opponent manly said that I had beaten him.

We made up after this, but I would not be so friendly to one of his countrymen who wanted a fight with me one night after a party. He was mouthing off what he was going to do to me, so off we went for a game off fisticuffs. A couple of lads came to watch as I smashed his head against the slabs several times. The watching lads then stopped this when I was getting carried away. I didn't like this bloke much so when asked, I told the lads I had given him a good hiding but as I was sitting in the bog having a Richard the Third I could hear him bragging to his mate on how he'd just kicked my arse so I wiped my arse (which he supposedly kicked) and popped out of the bog to his surprise, and then smashed his little lying head against the sink turning it from a brilliant white to a scarlet red.

We all went home on our leaves telling all our civvy mates the great times we were having and the life we were learning. Thorn and I decided to visit soho on one weekend. Young 17/18-year-olds being let loose on Soho in the early 80s.

We had a walked around then tried out these 50p peepshows.

There were about 12 doors leading into 12 booths, which all faced a square show floor.

So off we went into our booths. My 50p would not work so I started to panic. "I'm going to miss the show, my 50p won't work," I shouted out to Thorn. "Use the one next door" he replied so this is what I did. A little old bloke had just walked out, so I quickly jumped in. It was dark in there, but I managed to get the 50p in the slot and down popped a flap. I moved my feet forward to get a better view; the floor was all wet and sticky under my feet as I put my eyes up to the rectangular hole in the wall. Through the hole I could see this fit bird undressing, music coming from inside and then she put on a show for everyone. She approached my rectangular hole in the wall and then shoved her hairy beaver up to where my eyes were popping out of my head, she asked me to shove some notes through the hole and she would give me a good viewing. At first, I shit myself and moved my eyes away but then I moved back. She was now over near Thorn. "Get a load of that its fucking tasty, isn't it?" I shouted out to Thorn. "Stick your fingers through, see if she will give you a smelly finger," I then shouted but then my 50p had run out I searched my pockets frantically, but I had no more 50p pieces so I opened my door and went outside. There were other doors opening with these Japanese people coming out with big smiles on their faces laughing and chanting away together. This old lady then pushed passed me and went into my booth carrying a mop and bucket.

Thorn then came out. I said, "What's she doing?" pointing to the old lady with the mop. Thorn then said that all them Japs were having Thomas Tanks in there. We then left looking for more fun, me wiping my shoe in the grass first.

We came across a club. TOPLESS WAITRESSES, STRIP SHOW. "What you reckon?" "Might as well!" We paid the doorman a couple of quid and went down the stairs entering an empty club. We sat down watching these crap porn slides on a wall. The waitress then came over to us and asked what we wanted. "Pint of bitter and a pint of lager," we replied, "and ain't you supposed to have your tits out?" "I will get my tits out when the show starts," she said.

We sat there then watching these shit slides on this wall. I would have rather had a porn mag in front of me.

Still no strip show, then back came the waitress with our beers, "That will be £20 then lads please." Thorn looked up at her straight face "You're having us on aren't you?" in his southern accent

"No. its £20 lads, that's what it says on the price list," as she shoves the price list into our faces. At this point she is joined by this big black girl (she hasn't got her tits out either). "Got any problems?" she asked the waitress. "Yes, they won't pay." The big black butch bitch looks down at us two and says, "Two big smart lads like you down at Soho with no money, come off it." "I swear I'm broke," I said, so she searched Thorn took £8 off him and took my beer off me. "Fuck this,", I said, "drink up let's go." As we were leaving, we looked over and the two bitches pulled up their tops and showed us their tits as they were laughing away. "Fucking shit tits you fat cow, fucking day light robbery, no topless waitresses, no strippers, we will be back with the battalion and will burn this fucking place down," we shouted. We got upstairs, gave this old guy a hard time on the door and then went back to the peep show before returning to the barracks.

We finally finished our training and had a big passing out parade where all our families came down and watched us. All our parents wearing the best clobber being as proud as punch of what the army had achieved. All the lads then chipped in a tenner each for each instructor as a special thanks. Corporal Stone got an envelope with jack shit in it.

We all said our goodbyes to our jock buddies before going home with our family on leave.

CHAPTER 2

New Draft

When we got to the battalion Thorn and I were delighted, as we were both in the same company and the same platoon.

We were all given new extra kit, which we would be needing, and then given some training before we went to our companies.

Thorn and I were in an 18-man room. This room was carpeted unlike the polished floor in training; it also felt warmer and friendlier.

I remember having to walk to the end of the room where our beds were. All the older soldiers were sitting on their beds cleaning their kit but all staring at the two of us. Thorn looked at one who asked Thorn, "What the fuck are you looking at?" I thought, that's a nice welcome.

We were the new draft and it was common practice to give the new draft a hard time.

We had to retrain and now gain the respect of the older soldiers and be part of this new team.

We were at the end of the room because that was where the television was, and our fellow comrades would watch this all night while we tried to sleep. Sometimes, there would be empty cans of pop and crisp packets thrown into our bed spaces and every morning the floors had to be swept so the lads would sweep out their bed spaces then push the rubbish down to our bed space as that is where the bin was, and then Thorn and I would have to clean up all the rubbish.

We did not have to have the army itchy blankets. We could have our own quilts. We had a bit of privacy as well with the two lockers on one side of our bed then the next bloke's lockers giving us our own bed space. We could put posters on the walls, have our own armchair and rugs.

We had all the shit jobs but that was all part of being accepted and part of army life, it would only happen until we got some more new draft.

The old pranks would come out as well and would keep coming out every time new draft joined the battalion.

When you were on guard at the Tower of London you were made to do the ceremonial of the Ravens. What happened here was when the Tower was closed from the public; the new draft would have to get changed into our number ones. We would then be marched to where the Ravens were. We would be carrying a tray with bread on it, halt at the Ravens, and then on the count of three toss the bread to the Ravens and then place the tray under our left arm, salute the Ravens and then about turn and march back in.

We would be sent to count the pigeons as the sergeant had signed for 12 but we would never be able to count 12 so we would be sent to search for the missing ones.

We would be sent to the master tailor and would ask him for a long wait. He would say OK stand over there. After about ½ an hour he would tell us to go.

We would look at each other and say what we going to do, we haven't got a long wait, so that the sarge can stretch his buff belt? It took a long wait a while to sink in.

We also got sent to the stores and asked for tartan paint as the jocks had run out.

Skirting board ladders was another one, but this was all about being the new draft.

Back in our room, one of the older lads was very strange and could be heard at night. He would say goodnight to his bedroom furniture every night. The lights would be off and everyone in the room would be just nodding off and then you would suddenly hear "goodnight locker," "goodnight chair," "goodnight pillow," "goodnight bed," and some nights he really went for it. "Goodnight trousers," "goodnight boots," goodnight tie," etc., etc. This lad didn't go out much and was a bit of a loner (wonder why).

We were also told of the old Chinese saying "Sleeping man does not move faster than falling white locker." This being a warning to us that if we were not up to standard the white locker could always somehow accidentally fall on us when we were sleeping.

What Thorn and I had decided was that if during the night anyone tried to fill us in or anything then we both would stick together.

The older soldiers soon took to us and we went out on the piss with these quite often. We were taught the three 'Ss' that we had to do before we went out and the three 'Fs' or if you were going to be romantic, then the four 'Fs'.

What the hell are the three 'Ss' and 'Fs' I hear you say? Well, its first a Shit, Shower, and Shave and then we go out and Find them, Fuck them and then Forget them unless we want to be romantic then it's Find them, Finger them, Fuck them, and Forget them!

Thorn and a few of the other lads often came home on leave with me but it seemed every time someone came home to mine, we always seemed to get into a fight. We would go back to the barracks with either cut faces, black eyes or sprained fists. It was good then as you could go home have a fight, kick the shit out of someone or got the shit kicked out of you and nobody knew who you were.

On one occasion, Thorn came home with me and we stayed clear of fighting and instead pulled these right two slags. It was the middle of winter (snowing) and we got off with these two at the local night club, which was quite empty for a Saturday night, the nightclub was very smart with two floors, the dancefloor being in the middle with several well stocked bars and several seating bays with tables. With it coming to the end of the night we had no choice but to take the girls back to their house. As we were all lying on one bed, I asked if anyone fancied an orgy? Thorn was up for it, but the two girls were not. So off I went with mine upstairs. We went into her bedroom, which was dirty, and cold, we climbed over a couple shagging on the floor and got into bed. I then got myself a couple of smelly fingers then added another. After about ten minutes I jumped on top of her and slid myself in. I started banging away and she just lay there so I thought I bet I've slipped out and I'm fucking her thighs and cheeks of her arse, so I asked her. She said, "No you are inside me," and then started panting and moaning, anyway I shot my load and like any good man I rolled over and got my head down (sleep I'm on about). This was definitely the four 'F' but it was like putting a matchstick down the Thames. We left in the morning said our goodbyes and walked through the snow back to my house.

We were on guard duty the next weekend so we could not go home on leave. We were both on guard at Buckingham Palace. By now we had done quite a few guard changes.

The night before the duty we decided to go out on the piss, and both ended up shitfaced.

In the morning we all put our kit on the wagons (four-tonners) and boarded the coach.

We were based in the old barracks of Caterham, As the long journey got under way to London, I was feeling the worse for wear and felt sick and had decided that if I was going to be sick then I would be sick on the floor. I was holding it in very well but as we approached the Thames, Thorn, who was sitting next to me in the window seat, let roar and was sick all over his number two dress and into his bearskin which was on his knees. He then threw up for the second time splashing this lot against the window and covering the corporal sitting in front of us.

All you could hear was "You dirty bastard," "The new draft's pissed," "It fucking stinks," "Lock him up." The sergeant major told someone to pass a bucket and Thorn was sick in that.

Then it was my turn. I pulled the bucket off him and started throwing up in it. "They're both at it, dirty bastards." "They were on the piss last night. Lock them both up, his mates only come out in sympathy for him."

After we had finished the sergeant major started firing the questions at us. "Did you two go for breakfast?" "Yes sir," (it is an offence to miss breakfast). "Were you two out on the piss last night?" Thorn replied, "No, sir we went to the pictures last night." "What did you watch?" Thorn once again gave the answer to a film, which was on and then said I think it was something we ate sir as we got a Chinese from the Chinky outside the gate's sir (there was a Chinese and chip shop just outside the gates).

A voice piped up from someone on the back seat; "I've had the shits after eating one of their meals." Someone else also said the same, someone said they had been sick. The sergeant major sat back down and said he would see us later, all we needed to do now was get through the changing of the guard without fainting, which we just manage to do.

Another time when we were on guard duty at Buck House, Thorn was on duty in the back gardens and I was on duty at one of the side posts, there were also other officers on stag at their posts and there was those who were in their scratchers getting some sleep as it was around about 2 am.

It just so happened that the lads in their scratchers were the old soldiers.

I was doing my patrol, walking around thinking about this and that. Suddenly the guard was crashed out.

The police and not to impressed old soldiers were all running around to the rear gardens of Buck House. Weapons in their hands.

Nobody knowing why the guard had been crashed out at 2am, it must be something important, an attack on Buck House? An Intruder?

It was Thorn, he said he had seen someone come from the rear of Buck House near the swimming pool and run across the gardens.

The lawns had sensors all over them and none of them had triggered off, nor had any of the other many alarms.

The grounds were searched, and nothing found.

The old soldiers mumbling what they were going to do to Thorn for spoiling their much-needed beauty sleep.

A police officer then walked over. He was older than the rest with greying hair.

He then started asking Thorn some questions.

PC – "What did she look like?"

THORN – "Long brown hair, wearing a long bright red evening gown."

PC – "Which direction did she come from?"

THORN – "Over there by the swimming pool end, running across the patio area."

PC – "Where did she run to?"

THORN – "Across the lawned area and away over there," Thorn pointing in the direction that she had run.

The police officer took everyone by surprise then and said, "Yes Thorn did see something. That's our ghost, we have a couple and she pops up every now and again."

To Thorn's relief he was then let off by the old soldiers who then went on about the ghosts they had all seen whilst on duty at the Tower of London and Windsor Castle.

We were still the new draft when we were sent on our first deployment to the Falklands.

Before going we had several exercises, getting us ready for what we might expect when we got down there.

On one day we would route march from place to place using our navigation skills. When we had reached where we were going there would be tests. First aid tests, weapon tests, NBC test, airplane/helicopter recognition tests and many more. I remember this for one reason. I had just messed up on one of the tests and my platoon commander was giving me a real earbashing. He had told me to do something one way and I thought it should be done another way. Any way I did it the way he said and messed up, so we lost some points. After the earbashing, he said, "What's your IQ?" I looked at him puzzled and said, "What is an IQ sir?"

With this he looked at me shook his head and said never mind.

We travelled by plane to the Ascension Islands and then by ship to the Falklands.

Whilst waiting on board at the Ascension Islands, we all took up a bit of fishing. Trying to entice the hammerhead sharks, which were circling the ship.

We first caught the triggerfish, which swam near the ship. They would eat anything from sweets to my smelly socks.

We caught loads of these (who were something to do with the piranha family, with lots of razor-sharp teeth); they even ate the dead ones that we had thrown back into the sea. What we did then was try and catch some tuna, then throw these along with the trigger fish as far out as we could, on some string and try and catch the hammerhead sharks. This kept us all amused for a couple of hours but as you can guess, we didn't get our hammerhead.

The ship we were on was an old cruise ship for the school kids (the Uganda).

We would be on this for 14 days. The morale got worse the longer we stayed on the ship. The lads would be thinking of their girlfriends and wives and what they would be doing on the Friday and Saturday nights as we were losing our money playing at cards.

When the sea started getting rough, the lads had to quickly learn the rules of the sea and the main one they were learning was not to be sick into the wind or stand down wind of someone being sick.

(On exercise once we were all washing and cleaning our teeth in this stream and there up stream was a couple of the lads – unknown to them that we were down stream, pissing in it.)

We hit a storm one day; the ship seemed to be sailing on its side. The waves were higher than the ship it was a Force 10 storm we were told. So, what do we all do? We all go into the bar wearing our life jackets drink beer saying our goodbyes to each other while watching The Poseidon Adventure on video.

We got to the Falklands safe and sound. It was something like out of an old black and white films as we approached Stanley Bay, the sea mist started to clear, and we could see the rocks and coastline of a cold desolate place. After disembarking, we was then flown by helicopter around the island to West Falklands where we would be staying. On land we all made our living quarters the best we could.

There were eight of us sharing a room, or should I say hut. There were two bunks at either end of the room, in the middle we had our lockers and just in front of these opposite the door was a small coffee table and a couple of plastic chairs.

Porn covered our walls, ceilings and in my case under the mattress of the bloke I was sleeping under in my bunk. We did a lot of training and minefield clearing and got drunk in the Naffi on snakebites. One night we were all shit faced on these snakebites and returned to our rooms and got our heads down. The next morning, I woke and looked up at the naked women on my porn art, looking down on me. I then noticed a wet patch and lied there thinking on how it got there. I looked down at my manhood and for a couple of minutes my mind was in confusion, did I shoot my load up there? No, I couldn't have. Did I have a piss? No, my mattress would be soaking. Then a couple of drips landed in my face running down into my mouth. "Nish have you pissed the bed?" I asked the lad who had the top bunk. "Yes" was the answer I received. You dirty bastard I shouted as I jumped out from under his bunk wiping my face.

Nish being a good friend of mine a handsome looking lad, about 6ft and well built. The girls loved him, but he was in a steady relationship. Like Thorn I had joined up with Nish and gone through our basic training together.

We also caught one of the lads one day singing his heart out into a tape recorder to send home to his beloved girlfriend. 'Careless Whispers' was the song and the whisper soon got around the camp with everyone taking it in turns to rip the piss out of him.

Being good mates, we took the piss out of each other any way we could. I knew a lot about Thorn as we had now known each other for a long time. I also knew about his girlfriend at home in England, I knew where she drank, shopped etc., etc.

So, I forged a letter to him from her as he had told me he had not received a letter for a while not even a blue-e.

Blue's being the free mail service that we received. A blue sheet of paper that you wrote on and then folded up and posted.

His face lit up on the morning mail call as his name was called out. You could see the smile come across his face like a Cheshire cat.

The blue-es were given out and the odd letters and then Thorn was given his letter.

What I had done was send him a Dear John from his beloved girlfriend, saying that she had found someone else.

Thorn then went off to his room to read his letter but returned to me about five minutes later looking terribly upset.

He said he needed to speak to me. So off we went to the toilets whereupon he held back his tears to tell me his love of his life had just binned him and sent him a Dear John. I instantly felt sorry for him and I could not take anymore and told him that I had sent the letter and explained how I had done it with a little help from the lads. He just stared at me and said nothing for a minute then said, "Some mate you are," and walked out not to pleased.

He never forgave me.

We also visited the locals on settlement patrols and were sent all over to clear minefields, clean up huts and make them into rescue huts. On one occasion, four of us and a couple of RAF lads had to go to this rescues centre and clean it up, so we were picked up in a Chinook helicopter and dropped off, the pilot told us he would be back for us in about five hours.

We cleaned it up and got everything sorted in about one hour, so we cleaned our rifles sorted out our kit and got our heads down. After about three hours, I got bored and started to explore and came across a cricket bat, so I shouted the lads and we searched for a ball. We could not find a ball but then one of the lads came out with a sack of potatoes. So off we went if any part of the potato was caught then you were out. The game lasted for about two hours and the time flew by; we all had had a great time. The chinook arrived and we all boarded it and took off, but as we looked back down all you could see was potato pieces all over the roof and grounds. Some clean up.

On another cleaning up job we did, we had to clean this hut up, as it was needed as an operation hut.

We tabbed to this hut, which was about 15 or more miles.

As we walked into the hut, the floor just moved full of mice, there was about seven of us so off we went trying to kill as many as we could. After about half an hour we stopped but we managed to only kill two mice. That night, nobody wanted to sleep in the hut and so we all set up our bashers and laid out our maggot bags.

Thorn and I were told by the old soldiers to set up ours away from theirs. So, we did. Then the old soldiers started cooking their supper, opening their compo boxes and cooking their bacon grills on their Hexi burners eating their oatmeal biscuits and boiled sweets.

It didn't bother Thorn or I as I opened my Bergen, pulled out a frying pan as Thorn got our rip-roaring fire under way, I then pulled out the fresh bacon, eggs and sausages that we acquired from the cook house the night before whilst on cook house duty. The bacon would have fed the whole platoon and not just seven of us.

We started cooking and the smell soon reached the old soldiers and before you knew it, they were all asking us for some, but we told them to get stuffed, kept the sergeant and our officer sweet by sharing with them and proceeded to stuff ourselves. On the next morning we still had loads left, so took what we wanted and shared the rest. Experience isn't everything.

We had live firing exercises and a lot of patrols and being still new draft any fires ablaze at night after the live firing. Thorn and I were always picked to be part of the party to put these out. On one occasion we marched for hour in the pouring rain before putting out the fire that had started from shell fire from one of the warships docked in the sea. On the way back it went pitch black. The rain was pouring, and we were very tired. Suddenly the earth beneath me gave away and I had fell into a crater from one of the shells. I could not feel the bottom and the crater had filled up with water. I just managing to pull myself out using my SLR rifle and then felt somebody grab me from behind and pull me back into the crater. It was Thorn who had been following me. As he went into the crater, he grabbed out at me using me to get out. We did manage to pull our soaking bodies out of the crater and managed to find our way back to camp. Wet and cold and lucky not to have drowned.

We managed to get about an hour sleep before being woken to start our stag. This with us being the new draft.

I was soon sent on a navigation course. We had to go from San Carlos Bay to Port Stanley in three days. This was because it took the Marines three weeks to get there but as I kept saying the difference was, they were being fired at and at war, unlike us.

It was 90 miles all in all. I met up with the rest of the lads and we all got on well. There was 'B', a 6ft3 skinhead. He introduced himself to everybody by showing them his tattoos, a swastika on his bell end and the words "SUCK DONT BLOW" on the base of his cock, then under his navel it said 100% white. These where his prized tattoos however he was covered. I said, "I bet them on your cock hurt?" he smiled, said, "No I love pain, I love to be whipped and tied up by my women."

('B' was a true squaddie and I met up with him again in Canada on the coach to Edmonton. We had all been out drinking and quite a few of us needed a piss. So 'B' just passes his pint glass around for people to piss in and drinks it. I have only seen this done once since and that was a bloke in our rugby club.)

We finished the course and made it to Port Stanley in three days then went out on the piss in their two pubs, where upon I once again got into fisticuffs with a sailor who then went running off saying he was off to get the shore patrol (navy police).

Whilst on tour we had many group acts sent over to entertain us, from Bob Carolgees and Spit the Dog, to Jim Davidson. Jim being a top bloke, when he was supposed to be entertaining the officers in the Officers' Mess, he kept getting away and joining us in the Naffi and when we nearly got crashed out to search for some soldiers who had gone missing, Jim was there ready to join in with the search. Wearing his combats and asking which helicopter to jump on.

The soldiers however were found before the helicopters arrived.

We did our six-month tour and returned to Britain.

On the subject of tattoos, one lad in Hong Kong gave himself a tattoo on his neck. He put his first name on his neck. (Hoping never to forget it.)

'ANDY' was his name but the classic mistake he made was doing it in the mirror and in the mirror, it read 'ANDY' but on his neck it read 'YDNA'.

He kept it on his neck for about a year before it was removed. Paid for by Her Majesty the Queen, I think.

CHAPTER 3

No Longer New Draft

After our long-deserved leave, we returned to the barracks where upon I was glad to find that there were two lots of new draft waiting for us all.

So, they then had the beds at the ends of the room, the television on all night in their bed space, the rubbish swept to them every morning and all the shit jobs. It was now my turn to teach these lads the three 'Fs' and 'Ss' and start to become the old soldier.

We took the lads out, taught them how to be wasteful with their money, while we saved ours. We came back from the being on the piss, walked past the chip shop then woke up one of the new draft and sent them down to the chippie to get us all chips while we made ourselves comfy on their beds whilst watching television.

We had a Geordie new draft called Ted. He had a strong Geordie accent and a young lad with ginger hair, spotty face and large build.

One night we returned from the piss, woke him up, and gave him our orders (now and again we would buy them a scallop or fishcake for their troubles). I asked Ted for chips and a can of clack (clack in squaddie terms is drink). He returned about half an hour later started giving everyone their food and then handed over my chips, "Where's my can of clack?" I asked. "They had Coke, Pepsi, lemonade, orange but they didn't have any clack flavour! I even went to the off license, but they didn't either," replied Ted. So, I informed him what clack was and sent him on his way again!

The whole platoon went out one night on the piss. (A couple of weeks earlier a few of us had got into a fight with a group of civvies, after getting the better of these, they ran into the pub returning with pool cues and started to go about us with these. We couldn't do much, I had one pinned in the corner and was giving him a right hiding, but the cues were smacking me on the head and back so the best thing I could do was leg it with the rest of the lads. The civvies chased us but we were all fit as fuck and left them behind. The next morning, we showed each other our injuries). We did not find the civvies from our earlier battle so just enjoyed getting pissed. Ted said he wanted a pizza and said he would buy me one. I said what about the rest of the lads; we had all come out together? So, Ted said he would buy them one too.

We were walking around looking for a pizza place when we walked past this nice Italian restaurant. I said they would sell pizzas in here, so we all went in and the waiter sat us all down.

We were sat away from everyone else in a room on its own next to the window, sitting around a long table with a white tablecloth on it. You could just about hear the faint music in the background.

Ted was showing off a bit, thinking the lads would like him better for splashing out his money, so he called the waiter over telling him drinks all round. We all had shorts and knocked them straight back. We showed Ted our empty glasses and in a big broad Geordie accent, he shouted the waiter "Manuel, Manuel," and said he didn't want to see any empty glasses on the table (which was fine by us). The waiter then brought over the menu (no pizzas) so I had chicken, potatoes, carrots and cauliflower cheese (this was £2 just for the cauliflower), the rest of the lads ordered what they wanted while Ted was ordering the waiter to fill up some more glasses.

The waiter then asked if anyone wanted a starter. I said I would have a prawn cocktail, one of the lads said you cannot have one of them. I said I love them. I must have one, so someone said well I will have a soup another asked for a prawn cocktail and in the end we all had starters.

We kept the drinks coming and got Ted more and more steaming. We then finished and told Ted to get the bill. The waiter brought over the bill and handed it to Ted while the rest of us looked out of the window talking about the nice two girls walking past. Ted soon sobered up, over £100 in the 80s was a lot of money, he could not believe it. He moaned a bit but as we pointed out he offered. We said we would sort him out for drinks in the nightclub (that would not cost much he was already ready to drop). Ted then produced his new visa card and paid for the meal. (He later had his visa card retained by the bank.)

Another lad put his visa behind the bar one time when our money had run dry. His bill quickly run up and the bank retained this as well.

We all went out quite a bit together, once to Southend where we left one boat afloat in the boating lake, would not get of the go-karts thinking we were all at Brands Hatch and ended up being escorted back to the station by the police.

We all got off with the local girls. Two took me and Ted to a hotel for a gangbang however we did not get in, so my girl was driving her automatic whilst giving a hand job (Thomas Tank) we then went behind a local pub where we all had sex in the car.

Another time Smudge and I got off with two classy birds that were well up for it. They took us back to their house and said they wanted us there and then. (Smudge was a handsome looking lad with dark hair and very stocky, always well dressed and had the gift of the gab with the girls.) We did not want to disappoint the girls so went straight into action with all guns firing.

The house was very nice and very tidy, well decorated something, which we hadn't been used to.

We stayed the night and in the morning my girl went off to work so I walked into Smudge's room wearing a lady's dressing gown. I then removed it and jumped in bed with my mate and his girl. She said she wasn't up for it and sat up, Smudge pulled her back down and I said, "Come on its every woman's dream to sleep with two blokes, you must of thought about it before." She then took us both by shock when she said she had thought about it before but now it had come to it she was scared! We did our best to comfort her then Smudge started kissing her, so I then let my finger do the walking. I then moved behind her and started to make my entry, while Smudge was getting a gobble, I was concentrating on what I was doing but then I looked up at Smudge; I could see him biting the pillow trying to stop himself laughing. I quickly grabbed the other pillow and started biting it but could not hold in my laughter. The girl then said, "You bastards," as we both filled the room with laughter. I said I was sorry, but I had the giggles. We carried on. Everywhere my hand went, Smudge's was already there. I then moved up to her mouth as Smudge took her from behind punching me in the back and playing up like two little kids. Smudge then stopped and moved his hand over her bum. She looked back and said what are you doing as Smudge started squeezing spots on her bum and then carried on. The girl told me she should not have done it after we had finished, I asked if she had enjoyed it and she said she had but felt a slag now. I said she was not and later that day she told me she was no longer bothered. I asked if she would ever do this again, she said she would not but then again if it was with Smudge and me then maybe she might. But she did say she was embarrassed when Smudge started popping spots on her behind.

I went steady with another girl after this; however, I do not think her mother liked me because in two nights she had called me a 'Thing' and 'It'.

We were becoming real squaddies now, going into nightclubs where it was £18 to get in with all drinks and food free. The women were beautiful, but we had just paid £18 entrance fee and we wanted our money's worth, so we would order pints and shorts at the same time and by the end of the night, we would be out of our heads. No girls just steaming.

Most other nightclubs we went to, we usually managed to get ourselves barred.

There was also Smudge 2, a fattish lad for a soldier. He was in another platoon and seemed always to be in the bath. Whenever you went into the toilets in the evenings, Smudge 2 was having a bath.

The toilet was spot less as this was part of our daily cleaning. There were about four piss troughs and four toilets for sitting on. There were sinks along the wall on your left as you walked in and three baths which of course had doors and walls around them, however the walls did not go all the way to the ceilings. The floors were painted and needed polishing daily, as did the brass pipe work.

Anyway, Smudge 2 would wrap his towel around him put his flip-flops on and walk of for his bath carrying his toilet bag and newspaper with his magazine hidden inside.

One day we decided to sneak up on him and catch him in his act.

So, we silently moved in on our prey carrying the two buckets of cold water. We got on each other's shoulders and popped our heads over the wall. There was Smudge 2 lying in the bath full of bubbles, legs up at one end and a porn book opened up behind the taps, Smudge2 giving himself a five-finger shuffle which soon stopped as the cold water made contact with his body.

Smudge 2 did not have much luck with his baths. Another time we all went around to a party around his girlfriend's house.

Smudge 2 was running his bath and we were all having a few beers. Phil a Geordie from number one company needed a shit and banged on the toilet door but Smudge wouldn't let him in. "Come on Smudge 2 it's me Phil I need a shit. Come on open the door, you tosser," said Phil.

Smudge 2 then opened the door saying, "Hurry up Phil my bath going to go cold."

The bathroom was full of steam and the bath full of soapsuds-cum-foam.

Phil must have then thought fuck it as he parted the soapsuds and shit in the bath then covered the soapsuds back over the bath, wiping his arse, opening the door and thanking Smudge 2.

Smudge 2 found his chocolate covered sponge.

Ted fell in love with an older woman who looked more like his mum than his girlfriend did. She lived in a shit flat and had a squawking baby. We tried to tell Ted she was using him but being a young lad, he would not hear any of it and he still would not leave her when she gave him crabs.

He noticed he got crabs whilst we were on exercise, so we made him have a bed on his own down at the bottom of the room and gave him his own shower. We then put a blunt razor blade on his bed and told him to shave his bollocks. He cuts himself to bits then went to the medical centre where the medical officer gives him some cream to rub over his hairs and that would get rid of them. (Too late Doc.)

Another lad had a penal wart. I found this disgusting, but he was proud of this, said it gave better friction and even named it.

CHAPTER 4

Overseas

The one good thing about the forces is you see the world. I've been to Falklands, Canada, Ascension Islands, France, Morocco, Hong Kong (Chapter 5), Singapore, South Korea (three times), Philippines, Malaysia (twice), Borneo (Brunei), Thailand and Northern Ireland.

After the Falklands, the next overseas posting for the battalion was an exercise in Canada. This was work, rest and play. We did a few different exercises, a platoon attack, company attack and finally a battalion attack. I was section 2 i/c (2nd in charge) for all of this; I would take my lads on an ambush or recci patrol.

Everything went well on the training and platoon attack or defensive and at nights we would return to the barracks and go off on the piss to the local town.

The company exercise was going ok. We were all attacking a hill I had just taken out a bunker with my 66 mm. This should not have been my job, however we found out at the last moment when I was giving the ammo out, that the new draft hadn't been trained on this yet so I said I would carry this and handed the 84 mm to the 84 mm team and the gimpy was with its crew. So, I had just taken out this bunker and the bunker had been cleared when we started to advance, and flares started to brighten up the sky and smoke grenades set off. The range officials then told us to stop the exercise. We all made our weapons safe, and all sat down. A helicopter came in and we were informed that one of the sergeants from another section had just had a heart attack. We were chuffed for two reasons. Firstly, it meant we did not have to scale this hill in the blazing heat and secondly, we found out the sergeant was one that was being a right arsehole anyway.

The battalion exercise went on ok until two soldiers were shot accidentally. I believe this had something to do with the Canadian officials messing up on positions or something but that was only rumour, this exercise was again finished early. I thought it as the Yanks who just shot or bombed friendlies.

We then had some R & R and were taken off to Edmonton for the weekend. We stayed in a hotel where there was a strip show on, so we all got changed and went into this bar. We sat through a really good strip show (not like the ones me and Thorn had been to in Soho) and then it was off to get ready for the night.

At night, we all went on the piss trying to split up from each other so we could pull and not just look like a group of squaddies out on the piss. I went with a couple of lads to this posh nightclub.

This club was big. It had two floors, balloons in nets on the ceilings, no fighting, no slags, nice people, everyone being friendly.

There were not any other squaddies there, so we managed to pull, and I pulled a nice little thing. Blonde hair, a beautiful figure and nice smile. After a while, we decided to return nearer to where we were staying and the girl, I was with said she knew of a nightclub, so she took me there and managed to get us in for free. But when we got there it was full of squaddies! All the company must have been in there. I was probably the only one who had pulled, the stares I was getting from the lads were laughable, but I was still with her, so I suggested we go back to my hotel. She was not up for this, being a nice girl, so in the end I told her I was lost! She pointed out the way for me to get back, but I then said I was not any good with directions, so in the end, she walked me back to the hotel. When we got there, she just followed me into the lift (I had got her hook, line and sinker). There was another lad in the lift who asked me for twos-up, I was always taught to share so I said OK. We then got to my room and went in. At first, she was not having any of it (nice girl) saying she just wanted me. Then I started with my spiel saying it was every woman's dream to go with two blokes and that if she went with us, she would be able to look back on it with fond memories. She started getting used to the idea and started to take off her jewellery (really nice girl), then there was a knock on the door. It was one of the lads I was sharing a room with asking why I had locked the door? I've a bird in here I shouted to him, so in he walks and says threes-up! I said OK but the girl was now getting extremely nervous. Then unknown in the corner we heard another voice from under the bedclothes, "I'll have fours-up"! Well one of the lads was by now getting really rampant saying he was just going to take her. With this I then said that is enough lads and kicked them out as by now this poor girl was shitting herself that she was soon going to have to find room for four big squaddies. After the lads had left, she said she did not want to stop anymore. Which was understandable and I became a gentleman and walked her to the front of the hotel where she got a taxi not realising that she had left her jewellery. On my return to my floor, I noticed about six lads queuing outside a toilet and said that they could use my toilet if they wished because it was empty. No, we have got a prostitute in here giving blowjobs! So, I pushed in the queue and waited my turn. The door then opened and one of the lads came out with a big smile on his face and I walked in.

Sitting on the loo was this blonde-haired prostitute about 45, naked, little tits and scabs between her legs. She asked if I minded if she could have a rest? I said no that is ok, then she asked if I could get her a fag, so I opened the door and asked one of the lads to get a cigarette. The word must have got around as now there was another six who had joined onto the end of the queue. With more coming. I gave her the cigarette and she started going on that this was her first time and that she was only doing this because she had two young children was unemployed and needed the money. She then put the cigarette out and said waved for me to move nearer to her, come on then she said as I dropped my trousers and she then moved her hand over my masterpiece and shoved it between her lips. She knew what she was doing and gave very good head and before I knew it, I had shot my load in her mouth. She then put her hand up to her mouth, spat my cum into her palm and then flicked it into the bath. I looked down into the bath and there was a pile of everyone's cum lining the bottom of the bath. With this she then asked if there was many more outside? I said no I think you are coming to the end, as I walked out the door and past the awaiting company parade. The lads gave her $15 for this, not even $1 a person.

On the next night, one of the lads came into me and threw me his keys. "There's a bird in my room, mate." So off I went and let myself into his room and he was right, there was a woman standing there holding a towel up asking me what I was doing in her room. All around the room was army stuff and she was trying to pretend this was her room. I said this is my room and that is my towel as I pulled it away from her revealing her naked body and noticing that she only had one breast. I did not want full sex. I did not know where she had been, but could imagine, so I asked her for a blowjob. She seemed happy with this as she told me to lay down and then proceeded by pulling my trousers and boxer shorts off and then started saying, "Please let me suck you off." I said, "Go on then." "Oh please let me feel that big willy in my mouth," I said, "OK carry on." "Please oh please I need it so much." I thought, "Fuck this," and pushed her head towards my cock and she then had her wish. She was just getting the rhythm going when the door swung open, and all the lads piled in laughing their heads off seeing me getting head from a whore with one tit.

We then returned to work and did some recuperation in Jasper trekking, through the Rockies and canoeing through them. The Rockies is breath-taking and it is the best scenery that I have ever seen. We canoed down the river and stopped up at this little town where we set up camp. The town was something out of *Rambo First Blood*. A little town with one sheriff and a couple of deputies. Only one bar that we hit straight away.

We went up to the bar with everyone staring at us and asked for four pints. The woman looked at us funny and said we only do jugs, so we said four jugs then! She looked at us funny and said you mean four glasses and one jug?" "No," I replied, "Four jugs." "Ok you want four glasses as well?" "No just four jugs please." "Take a table and I will bring them over to you."

So, we all sat down everyone still staring at us and she brought the jugs over. We paid for these and then grasped the handle and knocked back the jugs and ordered four more straight away. This went down well with the locals and they soon joined us trying their hardest to out drink us without any luck.

We returned to the campsite and one of the locals pointed out a caravan to us saying it was a Native American. So, at about one in the morning this poor Native American family had four drunken British squaddies dancing around their caravan trying to carry out Custer's Last Stand.

The next morning, we all awoke with stinking headaches and carried on canoeing down this beautiful river. (None of us had been scalped in the night.)

The next place I was off to was an expedition to Morocco. We were going to be filmed by Channel Four travelling through France into Morocco through part of the Sahara Desert down a river, where man had never been and then end up in Timbuctoo. However, the river dried up and Channel Four pulled out.

We still went on the expedition travelling through France in three Land Rovers, which had been painted white, four in each. We ended up in the Port of Sète and had a walk around the shops and bars while we waited for our boat. It was a hot day and me and my mate Nish, ended back at the land rover before any one so Nish said, "Fancy a swim?" I said, "Ok, then," so we both stripped off and dived in. We were swimming around for about 15 minutes when we noticed all the locals come out and watch us, some off them calling to us and waving at us to get out. The next thing, the police turned up and ordered us out. So out we got, and the police started giving us a bollocking in French. Our officer then turned up with the rest of the lads and he took over. He then found out the problem and gave me and Nish another bollocking calling us both 'mongs' as theses posh guards officers do. The problem was that we had both been swimming in the harbour, which was highly polluted, and the locals had been trying to get us out. The police wanted us to go to hospital but we both said we hadn't drunk any of the water, so they said we were ok to board the boat!

We got on the boat, which we would be on for two days. We were the only white people on the boat, all the rest were Moroccans or Algerians. We didn't have cabins and were supposed to have this upstairs room, but we were meant to share this with the Moroccans, who were slouched over all the seats, smelly feet everywhere, dirty nappies left on seats and on the floor and people openly cutting their toenails and leaving them all over the place. We managed to dodge bits of flying toenails using the skills we had learnt.

In the end it was sleep where you can, so we managed to get our own space on the deck.

The ship come boat had one bar and a nightclub which would suit us fine.

We explored the ship, looked at the scenery and played cards as we travelled south. At night-time, we all got ourselves a bottle of duty free each, drank these as we played cards then a few of us hit the onboard nightclub. We sank a few more beers then hit the dancefloor, 'Grease Lightning', 'Saturday Night Fever', Michael Jackson, Elvis, punk we showed the watching Moroccans how to dance. The slow music then came on and a couple of the lads fancied their chances with a couple of modern Moroccan girls but one of the men didn't like this and we ended up squaring up to him and his mate and had a heated shouting match without any fisticuffs. (Luckily.)

No more was thought about this until we left the ship and were waiting in the queue, to pass through immigration and then we saw this big Moroccan who we had the trouble with the night before walking down the queue checking passports. "Oh shit," Nish said to me as he pointed to the bloke who had also seen us by now. He pointed us out to his colleague and they then started ranting and raving at each other however his colleague in the end just waved us through.

They all knew that we were soldiers, they did not know if we were mercenary on our way down to Algeria where there were some hostilities going on

We got some supplies in Tangiers and then spent the next week and a half travelling through Morocco. We had an incident in every town we visited. In Marrakesh, a shopkeeper pulled a knife out and held it against one of our lad's throats. The lad Orville had seen this knife he wanted while we were in the market. I had haggled the shopkeeper down to a good price, then walks in our officer who once again, called us both 'mongs' as we wouldn't be able to get the knife through customs, so Orville said no thanks and started to walk out. Next thing we knew the knife was being held against Orville's throat with the shopkeepers English improving by 100%! "You bastards, you fuck me about, you no fuck me, you buy fucking knife, or you get fucking knife."

I looked at Orville, his feathers were getting ruffled, his trousers were beginning to fill up and smell as the sweat was pissing out of him like Niagara Falls. I then looked in the shopkeeper's face. "We millatare (military) you fuck with us we come back bang bang," I said pointing my gun fingers at him. This must have done the trick because he let Orville go and just said, "you go, you go," waving us away. Swearing and shouting at us as we covered each other's backs as we exited the shop.

Nish was a smart looking lad. About my height 5ft11, and about 14 stone.

A ladies' man, always the first to be chatted up. Always well turned out and not really a squaddie. He knew how to treat a lady and rarely got into a fight.

Orville, well Orville got his name because he looked just like Keith Harris's little friend Orville the Duck. (His name hasn't been changed because I couldn't think of a better one than the one we all know him by.)

He was all of ten stone, had big ears, small stuck-up nose and a protruding top lip. I do not think he had ever kissed a woman let alone do anything else.

We all took the piss out of Orville; even the regimental sergeant major would on parade. But it must have got to him one day when we caught him behind his locker door looking in the mirror at his ears that he had just stuck back to his head with Blu Tack.

We were left alone quite a bit, as everyone knew we were military. We travelled into part of the desert and stayed at a town on the edge where we played football with what seemed to be a thousand local youths who came from everywhere, they seemed more concerned on getting my Adidas shorts off me instead of the ball (queers).

We went into Rabat, where we were invited to the British consul's house. We showered there and then had some cans of lovely cold tartan bitter. We had been invited to stop in the grounds and set up camp, but Orville fucked that up for us when he showed the consul's wife his new blanket-come-rug that he had acquired. "That's very nice," she said in a nice posh voice, "how did you come across that?" "I swapped it for my hi-fi," replied Orville. "Was it a good hi-fi?" "No, it was fucked."

Off we were sent down to a campsite down the road.

We went to Algiers, which is the resort of Morocco and hit the pubs and clubs. We once again got into a raised debate with some locals in a nightclub but left without any incident. One of the lads had pulled and was off with his girl but was soon confronted by two big Moroccans down an alleyway both waving big knives, so what does he do? He does what any brave squaddie would do. He walks towards the smaller one; girl in arm then throws the girl at him and legs it. Well done mate! More than likely set up by the girl.

We all ended up in this nightclub one night. We had been on the piss all day and it was early in the evening We all just sat around this table, only had one drink, then the lads said fuck this it's shit, lets return to the campsite. "I'm fuckin staying here," I said, "I've just paid eight quid to get in."

Orville and Snappy stayed with me while the rest left. Snappy being a tall lad from Barnsley in Yorkshire, not really a fighter or a ladies' man about six foot, skinny not very handsome but always having a laugh and joke.

As soon as the other lads had left, the place filled up with the bar upstairs closing and everyone coming into the nightclub the place was packed. We watched belly dancers, snake charmers, the lot and then a nice little Moroccan came over to me and sat down by me. "You want to fuck me?" she said. As she grabbed my hand. "Yea wouldn't mind." "Your mate wants to fuck my mate?" she said pointing to Snappy. "Snappy, Snappy," I shouted, "you want to fuck her?" "Yeah," replied Snappy. "Your other mate wants to fuck her?" the girl asked pointing to another girl. A fuckin' orgy, I said. "Orville how about it?" "Fucking too right," he said thinking he was going to lose his virginity.

I then jumped up, "Come on then fuckie, fuckie lets go." "How much?" I stopped, looked down. "What did you say?" "How much you pay for fuckie fuckie?" "They're fuckin whores," I shouted to the lads. Anyway, I knocked her down to about £11 and we then went back to their place. Down these dark alleys through a broken gate and into a cold dormitory, whores getting fucked all over the floors. Fuck this for a game of soldiers, I'm off I said followed by the other two.

We told the rest of the lads about our eventful night and all went back to this club the next night. Some of the lads got off with the whores but our sarge and I moved in on the only two white girls in the club. Both were as rough as fuck and as fat as fuck. One being British, the other a Yank. We quickly chatted them up and went back to their apartment. The two-fat slags used the bathroom first whilst we finished off their Bacardi.

They then reappeared wearing down to the floor nighties (what a fucking state they looked) we then went into the bathroom, I shit in the bidet, the sarge stuck their toothbrushes up his arse one at a time! Then we wrote our names all over the mirrors with their toothpaste and then returned to the fat slags.

"Freshened up?" said my British tart. "Yeah, feel much better for that" as I started to strip off.

I then moved back the bedsheets and moved up against my girls, trying not to fall out of this single bed, As the sarge jumped in bed with his, the fat slags had turned the lights off so I fumbled around for a bit getting my sense of direction. Arse? No thigh, belly? No arse, belly? Belly? Fucking hell is her mate in bed as well? No that was confirmed as I heard a shout from the other bed "Get your hands off me you ain't getting any." I then carried on with my examination. Belly? Yep, tits? No arm. Tits? Yep tits as I then started sucking the gigantic mounds for Great Britain. I somehow managed to remove her nightie and then her hand moved down over my cock.

The next thing I knew she let go off my cock ripped back the sheets and on with the light. What is that she said pointing down to my cock. (Cheeky fat cow it ain't that small.) Then I realised what she was on about. The scab on my cock. (I had thought it was a touch of syphilis but got it checked out when I returned to England and it was only a friction burn.) Quick thinking me said "It's so hot out here that I don't wear any underwear under my jeans and the other day I caught my cock in my zip." "Oh," she said as she turned the light off and jumped back into bed. "I bet that was painful," she said as she engulfed my manhood licking the end and then sliding her lips over it and then taking the whole of my cock into her mouth. Later I found some talc, sprinkled this on her until I found the wet patch and then made love to her – no that is wrong I fucked her. In the morning, we woke jumped around the room doing moonies to the locals acting like two little kids before meeting up with the rest of the lads only to find two of the lads had shagged them the night before us.

We returned to Tangiers and boarded the ship and travelled north. We were allowed back in the nightclub, but we couldn't dance and had to sit there and watch everyone else. The club finished and Duck and I returned to where we were sleeping. (Duck came from the same city as me, he was about 6ft1, had blond hair and missing one of his front teeth.) Duck then took me by surprise as he picked up a fire extinguisher. I thought he was going to soak me, so I picked one up as well, but Duck just threw his overboard. You twat I said as I let rip with mine covering him in foam, the next thing I knew the crew came running around the corner, so I covered them as well and then we legged it followed by the soaked crew. I ran past a couple of our lads playing cards and dived into my sleeping bag. The crew caught up and started ranting and raving in Moroccan; I then popped my head out of the sleeping bag and saw these three, soaked, foamy crew pointing down at me. Shouting at me and then the lads playing cards, I said don't blame me I've been here all night (not realising that I was also covered in foam). They then went on saying I would have to see the captain and I would be arrested once we docked at Sète. To my surprise and everyone else nothing happened, and we passed through customs and travelled through France back to England, our officer not knowing what happened on board. This saving me from being called a mong again.

We then returned to England and told all our mates about the time we had. We then had to get the Land Rovers cleaned down and all the paint off before we were allowed on leave.

We wanted to make the best of our leave because in a couple of months' time we were being posted as a battalion to Hong Kong for a two-year posting.

I went home on leave and went out on the piss with my mates. On one night we pulled theses three nice girls and went nightclubbing with them, then got a taxi back to their flat.

By now I was getting quite good with the old chat-up lines and managed to usually get into bed with my girls on the first night and this was not using my line, "Any chance of a fuck, love?"

On this occasion I got off with the nice blonde bit. She told me that she had fancied me for a while and had been waiting for me to come home on leave.

I did not tell her that I would soon be leaving for two years but let her think that I would be around for a while and she had a good chance of seeing me on a regular basis.

We all sat in the lounge and got more and more pissed telling each other jokes and all that stuff. However, I could feel myself falling asleep and was getting really pissed. I then jumped up and said well I'm for bed anyone joining me? With this the blonde jumped up and said come on then and took me into her room.

We undressed and got into bed, I let my finger do the walking again, but I was feeling really pissed so I thought I would have a quick shag then get my head down, which I did. I do not think she was too impressed with my lovemaking but I'd shot my load and pleased myself so now it was time for some shuteye.

She was less impressed with me in the morning as I could hear her talking to her mate in the kitchen as the sun from outside was beaming through the window straight into my eyes, which I covered to try and stop my head pounding from the massive headache that I had got.

I lay there listening to the girls talk as one of them said, "Dirty bastard he just covered it with the bathmat."

I wasn't too sure what they were talking about, so I got dressed and walked into the kitchen. My tongue was feeling like Gandhi's flip-flop, so I said any chance of a brew.

The girls had told me my mates had gone off to work and handed me a cup of tea. They seemed to be ok with me and made conversation before calling me a taxi.

I said my goodbyes and said I would see them down the pub later.

I met up with my mates and we went to the pub. The girls were working behind the bar, so we sat down while Nigel got the beers in.

Nigel being a big broad lad with ginger hair nicknamed 'Nice Nige' do not ask me why.

He chatted to the girls and started laughing returning with the beers. "You dirty bastard," he said looking straight down at me still laughing. "What?" I said not knowing what the fuck I had done but remembering the girl's conversation in the kitchen. So, Nigel told me and then I even remember doing it. I had gone to the toilet and threw up all over the bathroom floor but because I was so pissed, I just put the bathroom rug over the sick and went back to bed.

I apologised to the girls who laughed it off and then got a rollicking from the one I was with as Nigel had told her I was off to Hong Kong. I said I would write to her and pay for her to come and see me, which she believed, like the dumb blonde she was.

As I was staying at my mum and dad's it was hard for me to do some shagging in the house, so I used one of my mate's cars on one occasion, but I dropped him in the shit as I had been shagging a long-legged brunette. We had reclined the seats and I opened my trousers pulled off her knickers and banged away for all of three minutes before I got cramp and binned this idea.

I gave my mate his car back thanked him, and we checked the car to make sure no knickers had been left or anything. When we were happy, he went off to pick up his wife. All was sweet for about three days then she noticed stiletto prints on the ceiling of the car, one hole and two nice prints on the nice white interior.

She went absolutely barmy at him saying she had suspected him of shagging it around for a while and that is it now, he can fuck off she's filing for a divorce.

He did manage to calm her down and told her it was me.

I then turned to nature and did open air shagging, which is very exciting, but not every girl likes this and not the girl I took home one night and bent her over, kneeled down and took her from behind in the fields near my house. I pushed her head down and we both enjoyed the pleasures of the night. The nice cool breeze blowing against our naked bodies. The girl then started to moan and groan and scream, I fought god I have a screamer here, she's loving it. however, it wasn't until after I had finished that I realised that I had only shoved her head into stinging nettles and her face was right picture the next day.

An old friend of mine worked on the door down our local pub, Bri who I had played rugby with since I was 11. He had a bit of a name for himself being the ex-leader of a skin head group and had a ten-inch skin graft done on his neck from and encounter with a group of mods and a glass. So one night I went to visit him and got off with yet another bird and took her to her car which was parked in the car park where we both groped each other for a bit. I then told her I needed the toilet so went back into the pub where the lads had asked where I had been, so I told the lads that I had a bird in the car before returning to the car.

The girl was happy that I had returned and then went down on me as I just lay back and thought how sweet this was. Looking out of the window looking at the stars.

I then noticed a head pop up at the window, it was Nigel's, then there was Bri, Ian, John and then the manager with his video recorder going. When they noticed that I had seen them, they all started to laugh and shake the car, the girl then rose her head, but I pushed it back into place to hide her identity.

The fun had stopped, I did up my trousers and said my goodbyes but taking her phone number first as she was a right little goer.

The pub was one of the first to get these new television screens, there were about 12 sets all next to each other and other single ones dotted around the pub. On the Wednesday, the lads dragged me down to the pub. Halfway through the night the DJ announced to the full pub that the music was going to be stopped for a couple of minutes so we could all watch a video tape. Yep, it was my claim to fame a good showing if I say so myself. Girls in the pub were looking over at me, lads were saying it is that lad over there with the doormen the one who's on leave from the army. I just stood my ground raised my arms a gave a bow.

Nigel had just got a house of his own after splitting up with his wife, so I telephoned the girl from my video and we met up. I then went to the pub saw Nigel asked him if I could use his house. He said I could but to use the back bedroom and not his.

We had a couple of drinks then went to Nigel's, he had given us his alarm code, so we went in thought we had turned the alarm off and went to bed.

Now there are quiet girls when you shag them, lively girls who want it everywhere, girls who moan and groan and then there's the girls who shout the fucking house down, scream like shit and rip your back to pieces, and yes, I had the latter one.

A right good fuck but I could not keep her quiet. We had been shagging for about an hour in every position we could think of, we had just stopped for a rest and I suddenly heard a knock at the door and then another knock so I put a towel over me and went downstairs opened the door and came face to face with two policemen. "Hello, do you live here?" I was asked. "No." I explained that it was my mate's house and I was on leave from the army and stopping here. The policemen were sound and said that they had received a complaint from a neighbour as they had heard a lot of screaming coming from inside and the alarm was going. We had not heard the alarm sounding due to her screams.

My video dame then appeared, and the police just smiled and left.

The next day the lovely old lady next door approached Nigel (who didn't know about our late-night visit) and said I'm so sorry for calling the police last night but I could her a woman screaming in your back bedroom last night and was starting to get very worried as it was very loud, and I didn't know if she was in some distress.

After finishing my leave, I had to return to my battalion, so I said my goodbyes to my family and friends before returning to set off for my two-year posting to Hong Kong.

CHAPTER 5

Hong Kong – My Second Home

What a place.

As we came to land at Hong Kong's dodgy runway, we all tried to get a first look at this marvellous place. Looking through the window you could see the South China Sea; the high raised blocks, skyscrapers, and the harbour with large ships, small tugboats and loads of junks. Small islands, then we seemed to just pass over the tops of housing flats we could see the roads full of traffic and then we were over the sea again now coming down onto the runway which came out into the sea.

Looking left and then right you could see sea on both sides. We then started to see land at both sides and then bump, the wheels hit the runway and we were finally down after just over 12 hours in the sky.

The first thing that hit me was the humidity and the smell. The weather was nice, and we soon met up with the advanced party who put our kit on the four tonners as we all boarded the white army coaches.

It took us about one hour to get to our barracks for the next two years. We travelled from the airport into Kowloon through the tunnel and onto Hong Kong Island. Through the packed streets, everyone on the coach just stares out looking at our new play area, not many talking just taking it all in.

It was just turning dark as we travelled along the coast road passing beautiful beaches and then onto our barracks. Windows open as we tried to get used to the humidity, at night it was still hot and sticky. We could then see our barracks as we approached Stanley. It was out on its own up a big hill that we would all do plenty of running up.

We went through the gates where the bottom guardroom was situated and then the married quarters were pointed out to us. On the right-hand side, these were just past the bottom guardroom. They had their own outside swimming pool and lovely apartments, and this was a no-go area for us single lads.

We then carried on up the hill past several big houses that would be the commanding officers and other officers. Still going up the hill we came to the commanding officer's office, the RSM's office and Adjutants. We then started to go flat no more hills. We passed the top guardroom then came to the Naffi, barbers' shop, guardsman's mess and corporal's mess.

Next, we came to a small roundabout where the tailor's shop was. This was not the regiment's tailor but a civvy one and I think we all had suits blazers, etc. made for us while we were posted there. Next were the cobblers and then we went right to three, three-floored barrack rooms. These were for the single soldiers. If you followed the road around, you then had the sergeant's mess and quarters and passed that some old ruins up a couple off hills which we also got used to on our mornings physical training sessions.

The sergeant's mess and top guardroom were opposite each other with the single men's quarters at the end and in between these was a large drill square, a swimming pool and changing room and our rugby and football pitches.

I was part of the rugby team going and going in to the second half of the season we were second in the league, but border patrols and other commitments meant we couldn't train as we wished and we had a terrible second half. I of course played for the battalion rugby team and was also selected to play for the combined services along with several of my teammates.

We also had our own range and ammo bunker. So, you can see it was a very big barracks.

We were all allowed several days to get acclimatised to the weather and conditions before starting what was to be our tour of duty.

Whilst in Hong Kong we were to do four ten-week tours on the Hong Kong–China border as well as many other duties.

When we were in England you mainly stayed in your companies, like in the Falklands we were on different parts of the islands so most of the lads would not see anyone from another company for say maybe six months, but in Hong Kong we would all start to get to know each other and instead of fighting downtown with someone from another company, you would be fighting side by side.

We all asked the advanced party where the best places were to go on the piss and they gave us a rundown on the best places, the buses to catch and any info, which we might need.

Our main job whilst in Hong Kong would be to be ready for any deployments that we may need to be sent to in the Far East. So we carried on with our normal training, route marches, weapon training, enemy reconsideration, physical training, combat training, first aid, chemical war fare and much more, also keeping up with our drill on the square marching and getting used to arms drill with the new SA80 assault rifle which was replacing the SLR. We carried out border patrol and did our guard duty of the barracks.

However, enjoyed many nights out on the piss down the Wan Chi.

Wan Chai Warriors

Our place was the Wan Chai, which was run mainly by the Triads, but they seemed to leave us alone at the weekends and let us get on with it.

However, they did not like it so much during the week and one of the lads in my platoon found this out on one Tuesday night after he had been out pissing it up, he was held to the ground by a group of Triads and beaten over his legs with bamboo sticks.

The first place we all started to go to was a place called the China Fleet Club but after a couple of months of us being rowdy they barred us all, then would only let us back in if we got a membership card with our pictures on which we had to hand in when we entered.

The best place where we used to meet up was a place called Crossroads, which was of course on a crossroads. There was a bar across the road; one two doors down, one next to that, one over the road etc., etc.

So, to make it simple the Wan Chi was packed with bars, strip joints and down the road were gaslights where the whores hung out.

One of our lads was on adjutants orders for bouncing a cheque to a whore.

Every morning after a night on the piss you would end up (if you had not pulled) in the Horse and Jockey where you could get a full English breakfast.

The Horse and Jockey being an oldish pub with wooden tables and benches and a wooden floor which would have looked better if it were covered with sawdust.

The landlady (if you could call her that) being British.

It was a regular place for you to go over the next two years as you would always find someone from the battalion in there that you could share a taxi with to get back to the barracks. You would walk in this place say at five-thirty in the morning and there would be lads asleep on most tables, an untouched breakfast in front of them and a pint of San Miguel or Carlsberg next to this.

We did have a problem though and this was every time a Yank ship or submarine came into port; we were not allowed in the bars that we had been drinking in for the past months or year. Sometimes if it was only a small ship or only one then we wouldn't be barred.

One of our first meetings with the Yanks was when a submarine came in. I can't remember the name of it, but they would remember us.

It was a Friday night, all the single lads who weren't on duty were out but once again we had been told on CO's orders that we were not allowed into the crossroads so we went to a couple of other places. Some Yanks came in and started some trouble with us, so we got involved and all gave it to them and before you knew it the military police turned up along with the Yank shore patrol and the Hong Kong police.

The club was shut down while we were taken out and names taken. I managed to get away and went down the Horse and Jockey where I met up with other lads.

I didn't really know the lads that well because they were from other companies, but I had known them in the past, recognised their faces so just said all right to them as I entered the pub.

It soon got back to us early in the morning, that one of our younger lads had been given a good kick in by the Yanks at Crossroads.

So, we decided that we were all going to go down there but then one of the single sergeants came into the pub and said he had just come from the Crossroads and the Yanks had all fucked off.

The next night came and once again we had been told to steer clear off the crossroads.

I then ended up at the H & J again and met up with some of my mates. I had been out with an expatriate girlfriend of mine, but she would not let me have the ride, so I met up with the lads.

I went into the pub and it was quite busy. There were some Yanks in there that seemed ok.

I got myself a beer and started chatting to a couple of my mates then this Yank came over and started talking to us. He was thin with short brown hair but quite tall, standing near him was another Yank that was thickset, very muscular, but shorter than the first guy.

He started chatting ok at first, but this soon changed once a few more beers had been drunk. He then started going on about wars and then turned nasty saying to me, "At least we have never lost a war."

I looked up at him and said with a raised voice "You what? Never lost a war?" "What fucking war have we lost?" He replied also in a raised voice, "the Falklands you fucker lost the Falklands." "The Falklands," I shouted as the pub went quiet. "We kicked the Argies arse. You lost Vietnam, you twat."

Suddenly the pub just went into song "1CG are on the piss again on the piss again on the piss again." Then other songs started coming out everyone pointing to the Yank. "You're a wanker, you're a wanker." The Yank then put his drink down and walked to the door, I thought he must have had enough with the piss being taken out of him and he was leaving with his mates. As he got to the door, he looked back at me and moved his hands, come on then he said waving me to him, goading me to follow him. So, off I went after him not knowing the whole pub was following me. However, we did not know that the Yank had planned this and all his mates stood outside waiting in a trap for us.

Outside the Yank stood his ground all his mates, they came out from behind the cars and other doorways, they had been waiting for him to goad us out. We were being ambushed.

"Come on you Fucking Brit Wankers," they said one of them smashing a bottle and hitting Downsie with it (a lad from number three company) cutting his head and sending gushes of blood from the wound. I then grabbed the Yank, smashing his head off the wall about six times, Mid and Marsh (some one company lads) got into two other Yanks and Charlie (sergeant, one company) giving it to another, Clive (support company) giving it another. Some of our other lads got involved. I remember being punched and falling to the floor before getting up again. We managed to get the better of most of the Yanks who managed to get to their feet before running off. The harder Yanks stopped, and we carried on the fist fight with these. There was a right little stocky Yank that just wouldn't go down, he was full of tattoos, a little battle-axe, three of us then started to give it him but he still wouldn't go down (reminds me of a girl once, she wouldn't go down on me either) then a taxi came past, so he was thrown in front of this. It was not going too fast, but he hit it leaving a big dent in the side, he went down and stayed down. We chased the rest of the Yanks away before returning jumping up and down shaking each other's hands and hugging each other.

Anyone would have thought we had just won the World Cup.

Downsie was about six-foot three, looked very slim and elegant, having dark hair and coming from the same town as me. Now wearing a nice new five-inch scar on his head.

Mid was about 6ft, about 14 stone, never one to talk a lot, even though he came from Birmingham, he had dark hair.

Marsh was very much like Mid and they were good mates, he came from Devon.

Charlie was about 5ft10 and about 12 stone, blond hair, blond tache and loved a beer and a fight.

Clive was mad; coming from London and always having everyone in stitches with the things he was coming out with and doing. He was about 5ft11 and about 12 stone.

In the next days to come, the shit hit the fan. It was in the *South China Morning Post* paper and we were told it also made the English papers. Coldstream Bastards, Coldstream Animals.

Downsie needed stitches and while he was in hospital some of the Yanks had told him that you Brits fight like animals and they had never had a hiding like this before.

The submarine was supposed to have sailed the next day but could not leave for a couple of days as half the crew were in hospital.

Next thing I knew my name was called out in the morning company parade. I had to go off with Fraggle and a couple of others from my company to see the drill sergeant.

Fraggle was called Fraggle because everyone thought he must have come from Fraggle Rock. He was a thin lad with curly hair and wasn't into fighting, but he was a sound lad.

Waiting up there were Mid, Marsh, Charlie, Clive, Downsie and a few more.

The drill sergeant called out the names and then mine. They are after you, he said to me you are the main one. Oh, fuck I thought, off to Colchester, end of my army days.

Colchester being the military prison in the UK.

We were taken by minibus to HMS *Tamar* where we were interviewed by the SIB.

I was one of the first to be interviewed, the officer behind the desk called me by my nickname and told me to have a seat. (I thought how does he know my nickname?)

Nothing in the office but a desk and three chairs. Grey walls with no windows, polished floor.

Then the old ranting and raving started (he did not call me a mong though) we know you're the main one just own up, who else was there? Come on save time who punched the ginger lad? I have not a clue I said.

He went on at me for a while reading witness reports etc., then he left the room and some else walked in. He also called me by my nickname.

"Fancy a fag?" No don't smoke. "Cup of tea?" No thanks. (Mr Nice Guy, Mr Angry routine.) Come on make it easier on yourself, don't take all the blame, who else was there? I don't know, I said, they are from other companies, I don't know their names, I said (which was true at the time).

So, you only know the faces, he said. Yeah that's right.

Well, I will tell you what I will do then. (Using my nickname all the time as if we are long lost buddies.) I will telephone your sergeant major up and tell him to arrange a battalion parade tomorrow morning; you can walk down and just pick out the faces.

I said, I think not but thanks for helping me out anyway. Right, he shouted, I want names tomorrow or else.

We spent most of the day there before returning to barracks.

The next day I was called up again. This time there were about six other lads with me. But no Clive, Mid, Marsh, Charlie or Downsie.

I walked into the office again. Again, my nickname used. Please sit down, right then I told you I wanted names so let's have them, I was unable to give any names so was questioned all day and told to look after myself and come back the next day with the names.

The next day I was called up again out of the company parade and again the drill sergeant telling me they were after me and again getting onto the minibus to HMS *Tamar*. Again, there were about five other lads with me and again no Clive, Mid, Marsh, Charlie or Downsie

I walked into the office again. Again, my nickname used. Please sit down, right then I told you I wanted names so let's have them as I've more info on you.

I then took him aback as I said I've got you a couple of names. (His face was a picture.) Once again being my friend, using my nickname. Good I'm glad you have seen sense; nobody will know the names have come from you. Right let us have them he said picking up his pen ready to write. Right, there was Kenny Dalglish, Kevin Keegan and Emlyn Hughes. I said. (He actually wrote down Kenny Dalglish.)

The pen was slammed down on the table when he realised what I had said. Do not take the fucking piss he said, calling me now by my surname.

What am I supposed to do, I said? Your witness is making it up (I know realised who the witness was) she does not like me and is making this all up because I wouldn't go out with her.

He then looked up at me and was silent for a minute before telling me to wait there a minute.

Returning a couple of minutes later he led me into this office. We entered a large office with another polished floor, chairs on either side with three officers on one side two RMPs on the other and the main man behind the wooden desk. A picture of Queen Elizabeth behind the desk looking down on me. A brass shell by the side of the desk and what looked to be a picture of his family on the desk.

The main officer then looked over his glasses and said, I understand you know my daughter? Shit I did not know it was his daughter. Yes, sir I replied. Taking it that the witness was his daughter.

You say my daughter is lying? Yes sir. "Well she has never lied to me in the past," he replied. Well, she is now sir, I said.

He then said, "Right I will speak to her tonight then." I looked at him and said, "Thank you sir."

I was led out and it was back of to the barracks. By now I was shitting myself knowing it was only a matter of time before I was going to be sent down.

I had even started packing away my kit and telling the lads to look after my television and my stereo.

Next day, company parade again and my name called out again, so off I went again another six lads in the minibus but there was Charlie going for a second time and me going for my fourth.

Into the office again. Surname used, no nickname and then to my surprise the officer said he had done some work for me last night and interview the landlady and had found out that I was not the one who had started it, and the main man's daughter hadn't even been in the pub.

I was the last one in this day and I think they had come up a blank as they said they were going to let the battalion deal with it now and report their findings to the battalion.

The ginger lad that they are basing the case on had been beaten up well before our battle by some else.

Next day Fraggle and I were on company orders the other lads on their company orders.

The company commander had Fraggle and I in together.

In we marched, left right, left right, left right, this being at some pace. It was then halt, right turn.

Us both now facing the company commander.

Our names were then called out as we took a pace forward trying not to bang our knees on the highly polished desk.

He asked Fraggle his side of the story. Fraggle said that he hadn't thrown a punch, the company commander asked me if this was true, I said it was and I didn't see him throw a punch. He then asked me if I threw a punch. I kept to my story that I had told to the SIB.

I said the truth about what had happened in the pub, then said the Yank left and a little while later Downsie left to return home, but as he left, he got glassed outside, I said I had saw this went to help Downsie and was helping him off the floor when I was punched. The company commander then said, but did you throw a punch? Yes, sir I said I was protecting myself and threw a few punches back before the Yank ran off.

The company commander then told me what a good record I had and what a good soldier I was. He then said if anything like this happens again, he would take me to the guardroom himself and lock me up. He then said case seen and we marched out.

One step back, right turn and again it was left right, left right, left right and again at some pace.

The other company commanders were not so supportive, and the rest of the lads were sent on commanding officers' orders. None got locked up, but all had to sign to say they would behave for the rest of the tour or be kicked out of the army.

They could not believe that I wasn't on commanding officers order too, and nor could I.

Later some of the younger lads had tattoo's saying Wan Chai Warriors. But they weren't the Wan Chai Warriors. We were.

Charlie, Mid, March, Clive, Downies and Fraggle are these lads' names and have not been changed. This is in honour of these lads and our new battle honour.

Not long after we were back at the SIB's office's again, this was when Charlie had been framed for something down the Wan Chai.

He had to go for an ID parade, so he picked out his mates to go along.

We all wore the same clothes, and all had blond hair, some with moustaches, some without.

We all stood there having a laugh and then were told to keep quiet and look straightforward at the glass.

We could hear the witnesses being led in and the speech was given to them.

"Don't worry, they cannot see you, it's a one-way mirror."

I piped up; "I can see you." Then someone said, "We know who you are."

Then the witness was asked to pick who they thought it was. "Number 2."

The next witness came in and was given the same speech. "Number 5."

The last witness called out Number 1.

It just so happens Charlie was not numbers 1,2 or 5.

No charges could be brought against him. Another win for us.

The Border

Like I said earlier, patrolling the Hong Kong–China border was our main job, along with being ready to be deployed anywhere in the Far East, while we were out in Hong Kong.

If you stayed in the same company, you would do the maximum of three patrols. I did all four patrols as I got promoted and moved to another company.

You had to travel up north to get to the border of Hong Kong and China, so we travelled up Hong Kong Island through the tunnel then through Kowloon and then through another tunnel into the new territories.

We would be taking over from the Gurkhas.

The border, this followed the Sham Chun River and there was also a road going west to east like the river. Then there was a 12-foot fence with barbed wire on the top of this.

The fence was alarmed and if anyone shook the fence, climbed the fence or tried to cut through the fence, the alarm would come through to the company's headquarters control centre, where a light would come up on the map on the wall of our company's position. The control room officers would then see which section was nearest to this and sends them.

In some places this system would be the same for a platoon location.

The company would be broken down into platoons along your company position and then the platoons broken down into sections.

At most high points you would have observation post. The main one was on top of a massive hill and had a concrete observation hut and then below this was sleeping quarters. There were radios, a telephone, binos, and two big two-eyed telescopes and at night there was the thermal imager, which would pick up any heat sources at night and helped us catch many illegal immigrants. This look out was so high up that you could see into china and the city of Shenzhen.

On one occasion when the cloud was low you would look out and could only see the tops of the skyscrapers in Shenzhen

On another occasion we had a storm. I was in charge as it was my stag and the sarge was getting some shuteye down at the sleeping quarters.

I was looking at the bad storm through the open windows when there was an almighty bang. We all hit the floor. "Fucking hell we are being shot at," I said.

We all lay there for a few seconds composing ourselves before I reached up to grab the telephone. I then got a shock from this.

We had only been hit by lightning.

"Fuck this for a game of soldiers," I said as we closed up shop and went down to the sleeping quarters.

They say lightning does not strike twice. Well, that's a load of bollocks because about a week later the same thing happened again, not exactly the same place but only a foot or two away.

Lucky me eh!

On your section posts you would have a hut with four bunks in, radios, water and cooking faculties and a couple of mountain bikes.

You had your own sensors, which you would put into the ground in places where you thought the illegal immigrants would come from. You had a receiver at your hut.

When the sensors went off you would jump on your bikes go to where they were and would normally catch an illegal immigrant.

The company or platoon would also send you if a zone had activated on the fence and if the observation post had spotted some illegal immigrants, they would move you into position and you would lie in wait.

The local villagers would also tell you if there were any illegal immigrants around.

You also had dog handler teams if needed.

The illegal immigrants only wanted to better themselves and their families.

We caught many on our patrols, some old, some young.

At first it was a real buzz waiting and hiding in the dark and then pouncing and catching these helpless people.

On one occasion we were sent in by the observation team. They told us to lie down behind this bank and then they told us, when the illegal immigrants were near, you would just hear, go, go move now. We all jumped up and climbed the bank, batons waving around in our hands, but we couldn't see anyone, as it was dark. The illegal immigrants had laid down but the thermal imager picked them up and we were then moved into them cowering in the thick wet grass and bamboo shoots. The best thing to do was just shout at them as they were shitting themselves and in a state of confusion.

We caught six this day two men, three women and a little kid. Another one had done a runner and had dived back into the river.

The next day we found him, the observation post told us to check out something suspicious in the river.

We then went back to the river near the point to where we had caught the others the night before to check this out and found that the suspicious thing floating in the river was a dead body. It looked like it had been shot.

There was about three of the Chinas People's Army on the other side of the bank trying to fish this out with a stick. They saw us gave us a wave then carried on. The Chinese often would shoot illegal immigrants.

Once we had captured the illegal immigrants, we would plastic cuff them then take them back to our section huts and await for the company or platoon to send vehicles and take them away were they would be searched interviewed and then handed over to the Hong Kong police before being sent back to China.

Some of the immigrants we got were in right states they had been travelling for days, weeks or even months.

Some had not ever seen a white man before and on one occasion this woman hadn't seen a white man or television, so we put her in front of a television. She did not have a clue what was happening.

We all learnt a little bit of Chinese, sit, stand, and a few swear words.

We also had to do our own physical training, so I just told the lads in my section just to make sure they went for the odd run when it was there turn off, but this backfired on me when they went off on a run up to see this old prozzie who had no teeth and was giving all the lads blowjobs for fifty pence (or equivalent). On their way back they thought fuck it and caught a bus but were caught by the company sergeant major.

I must admit I loved the border patrols and on our last one my section caught 53 illegal immigrants.

A Place of Beauty

Hong Kong was now becoming our home. I do not think there was anyone who was not enjoying their stay here.

We came back from our border patrols, did training, went on exercises and mostly enjoyed this beautiful place.

There was plenty to see if you were into that sort of thing. I didn't see much of the scenery until my second year when I thought I had better see more than just the inside of pubs and clubs but all I saw was the jumbo restaurant and went halfway up the peak.

I also visited Water World, a couple of beaches, the night markets and played rugby all over the island and Kowloon.

We spent two Christmases there and believe it or not I was not invited to anyone's house to celebrate Christmas, that was until Christmas day when my old platoon sergeant came walking around the room's and asked if there was anyone who had not been invited anywhere. I told him of one of the guardsmen but everyone else was OK.

He then told me to tell this guardsman to get his arse down his house for one o'clock and then asked me if I was going anywhere. I said I was not, but I was going to go down to the corporal's mess for a couple of drinks. He then invited me as well, so I sent the guardsman down to Stanley Market to get some presents for the sergeant's kids and went over to the corporal's mess.

I got a crate of beer and went down and had a nice Christmas dinner. Which I thanked him and his family for before heading off down the Wan Chai

After this I went down to crossroads where I met up with the lads.

Another Yank ship was in and we were allowed to go into our usual places. The week before I had my leather jacket stolen, this was a jacket that was my pride and joy which had been made for me by the local tailor. I knew it was the Yanks who had stolen it.

The Crossroads was packed, and I had acquired a CS gas tablet.

We used to do a lot of training for chemical warfare. Instructors putting us in a room and then sending canisters of CS in and we all having to say our name rank and number before being allowed to put the gas mask on or them throwing several tablets into my trench and telling us to remove our gas masks so I became used to this.

I am not saying how I acquired the CS gas but tonight revenge was being issued.

Most of our lads knew what was going to happen but not the Yanks.

The girl I was seeing at the time put the tablet in an ashtray then put a cigarette on top of this.

We then ran to the door and looked back, but nobody followed, and nothing happened.

We then watched from the doorway as several Yanks started to rub their faces. Then puff the whole place filled with a cloud.

People came running out coughing and spluttering. Yanks were running into the toilets washing their faces (which is the worst thing you can do; you just stand in the wind and let it be blown off you). After about five minutes our lads then returned down the stairs and nicked the Yanks' drinks. The place was cleared, no jacket but revenge was gained.

For about a month later a door charge was put on the door. The management said they would let everyone back in for free if they told them who did this. But the lads were sound, and nobody grassed me up and I was spared meeting this Triad gang,

Not long after this it was my 21st birthday. One of my mates took me out and we bumped into everyone.

Drinks were coming from everywhere but the one that I think done me in was the top shelf one I got from one of my mates, Manny.

Manny was a great bloke just looked and acted like *Emilio Estevez* from the *Young Guns* (Billy the Kid) films. He was always laughing, and the women just loved him.

What he would do if a woman was being not too cosy with him. He would sneak them into his room and put a video on. The video being *The Champ* which he had watched about ten times to harden himself up.

Then when the little boy went running around the table shouting "Champ, champ wake up, wake up, please don't die." Manny would then watch for the first tear and then move in to comfort the girl and the rest was history.

Anyway, Manny had got me this drink from the top shelf. There was everything in it and I had a pint of this. It was a horrible green colour and that is the last I could remember.

I awoke in the morning in my bunk for morning PT. The bunk stunk as I got out of bed.

I looked down at my sheets and had only pissed and shit myself. I walked out into the hallway still pissed. The lads could not believe it. Shit had stuck to my legs I was covered.

One of the lads then threw me into the shower, where I quickly cleaned myself up.

I did not make PT and was lucky to make it through the day.

We then started to find the classier places and had some good pub crawls. Mad Dogs, Ronnie Scott's and many more

One time we held up a coach and made the driver drop us off down at Crossroads.

We did not hold it up aggressively or anything we just stood in front of it and when the doors opened just piled in and asked to be dropped off en route. We had a right good laugh with the European passengers before getting off with them all waving us off some wanting to join us down the crossroads.

Downies and I went to a bar one night in Kowloon and after leaving the pub needed to relieve ourselves when we left, the toilet was full, so we just pissed outside the pub.

However unknown to us the place was another place run by Triads and this time it was also full of Triads, so the chase started. There were about seven Triads who chased us through the streets, we ran through the main streets, across roads, missing taxis and cars, downside roads, alleyways and then back onto the main roads dodging people as we ran, we kept looking behind us but every time we looked we could see the Triads still chasing us. It was like a James Bond film. However, after a while we looked behind us and only three Triads were still giving chase, we must have been running for a good two miles or so through the streets of Kowloon.

I was no longer as fit as fuck and noticed that they were not going to give up the chase, so I shouted to Downies (who was way ahead of me) to stop and fight them.

I stopped, looked around to see the Triads still coming then looked around for Downies who had kept on running. I was then face to face with these three Triads, all three smaller than me and all three ready and willing to see if I was up for the fight. I wasn't. I was caught and was taken back to the bar where upon was given a kicking by the Triads, but to be honest they went easy on me but I had to get on my hands and knees and clean up our piss before being released.

When I did finally meet up with Downies we did not see eye to eye. Downies said I should have kept on running and I said he should have stood his ground with me.

I ended up knocking out part of Downies tooth in the heat of the moment, but we soon made up as mates and to be honest, he was fitter than me and the Triads and I just could not run anymore.

Another night I was down the Crossroads and one of my section came over to me.

Franco, he was small with dark black hair and had been having a problem with yet another Yank.

The Yanks where here again and one of them had smacked Franco. So, Franco wanted to get revenge but there were several Yanks. As Franco's section commander I said I would come over with you and watch to make sure of no foul play.

I went over and stood at the back for a while as Franco asked this Yank why he had hit him. Franco not being a fighter, the Yank said sorry then they shook hands.

Great I thought that's OK then no problems, I can have a peaceful pint, but then the Yank said, "What's he fucking looking at?" Pointing at me. I asked what he had said as he approached me aggressively. I could see him going to start again then, so 'bang' I headbutted him before he could utter another word sending him flying across the floor.

His mate then came at me, thinking he could put a crafty punch into the side of my face, however I managed to dodge this onslaught and responded with left upper cut. With him landing on top of his mate.

There were people everywhere, lads trying to pull me off and lads trying to get a look.

One of my mates then said "RMPs" so I stopped went over to the bar and got a beer.

I then said to the English girl behind the bar that if anyone says anything then she's my girlfriend and he was starting on her.

However, we were not asked, the Yanks were escorted from Crossroads and my chat up line worked because I started seeing her from then on.

Before seeing her, I did get off with this Australian in one of the wine bars.

I had been out to one of the night markets with a couple of lads during the week and ended up in this wine bar.

This being a bit classier than Crossroads. Seating area only and a nice dancefloor.

Then in walks this stunning blonde. Everyone's head turns to look at her and then we get on with our drinks.

Next thing I know she says to me, "Do you mind if I sit here?" I said, "No." "Are you alone?" To which she replies "Yes" and then takes me for a dance.

The music was rock and roll and I was shit at dancing to this. Well shit at dancing full stop. Which she soon noticed and said, "Fuck you," and went and sat down. I think she thought I was taking the piss out of her with my dancing, but I am really shit.

The lads were all laughing as I sat down; I lost my dummy and went in a mood with her.

It came to the end of the night and I had not spoken to her since the dance, and I got up to go.

She said, "Are you going?" I said, "Yes." "You're not interested, are you?" she then said. "Look do you want to fuck me or not?" (Wow this was new to me I did not need to use my shit chat-up lines.) I said, "Wouldn't mind" and the next thing I was in a taxi with her going back to her hotel. She was all over me in the back of the taxi, "I want you to fuck me, I want you to fuck me hard, I want you to give me a real good fucking," she said.

This was new for me. "Hang on a minute, I've had a few beers you know." Think she is going to be too much for me. I'm only a young soldier.

We got back to her room and she told me to "Strip off." She was very dominant. She then gave me a can of beer and told me to sit in the chair. She then produced a camera and started taking pictures telling me to play with myself.

So, I had a can of beer in one hand and my cock in the other while she snapped away.

I then said it was my turn and told her to lie on the bed and play with herself, which she did. She had a lovely body, lovely waist. Legs and tits, with a Brazilian muff. I then used the rest of the film up on her, telling her to pose in different positions.

After this I lay on the bed while she tickled her tonsils with my cock.

She then said, "Right I want to fuck you."

I needed a piss so told her this. She went, "Fucking hell man, hurry up then."

I went for a piss and could feel something behind me so looked around and she was looking over my shoulder watching me piss then grabbed hold of my cock shaking it with my piss going all over the place and her laughing and squeezing.

We then went back to the bed where upon she mounted me.

She slowly inserts me into her but then pounds away.

Up and down she went on my shaft, "Am I good? Am I good?" she shouted as I was going "Aah, Aah, Aah." She got faster and faster. I was still squealing "Aah, Aah and Aah." "Yes, I'm good, ain't I?" she shouted.

She was not giving up and I couldn't take any more. "No," I said, "you've got my bollock caught." She had been fucking like a mad woman and my bollock had been caught up at the base of my cock it felt like I was being hit with a sledgehammer by her firm buttocks.

Next she said, "Come on jump, on give me a good fucking."

I jumped on but only lasted a couple of seconds before shooting my load. She was not impressed and was not afraid to let me know of her disappointment. "Fucking hell man, just fuck me. I want to be fucked, what's going on?" she said throwing a roll of toilet paper at me. I'm sorry I said, we could try again later.

I awoke later by receiving a blowjob. I looked down and she was determined to have her use from me this night, yanking my balls to make sure I was awake, when she saw that I was awake I was told to get on top and "fuck her" again so I did. "Yes, yes, oh yes, you're good," she said, "Oh harder, harder," she said as I was banging away like a rabbit, sweat pissing out of me.

This went on for a while and I was finding it hard to impress this rampant Aussie and soon got bored doing it in the same position. so, I started to pretend it was this girl or another girl still banging away.

She was there again, "Oh yes, yes, yes, you're good, oh yes, oh yes, oh you've gone soft," she said. "I'm sorry," I said, "but I'm bored doing it in the same position."

With this I then took her from behind and then she came, and I shot my load over her back. I think I might have pleased her and done Britain proud, some things just have to be done for Queen and Country.

In the morning I got the feeling that she wanted me to go as the lights were on, curtains open, TV on and radio on full blast.

She was walking around naked but banging around, she asked me if I could get her any work out in Hong Kong. She said, she would fuck to get the job, but not fuck while she was in the job. I said I would try and see what I could do. She then said well the truth of the matter is I'm over here from Australia for a week and want as many different cocks up me as I can. She then gave me a peck on the cheek while holding the door open.

In my second year in Hong Kong my best mate was a lad called Lumsey, a big 6ft2 plus lad, who played rugby, worked out on the gym and was a physical training instructor.

He was one of these blokes who pissed you off as he always looked like he had just walked out of a catalogue. Whatever he wore, whether it be a suit or shorts he looked smart. He was a right one with the women and all the classy girls wanted him.

Lumsey and me had sorted out our own pub crawl. We started off in the corporal's mess and then moved to the bar in Stanley, then went to Traps cocktail bar where you bought one, got one free.

We would stay there for about an hour then go over to Kowloon where we would pay to go into this bar which had free drinks for three hours and then move to another which had buy one get one free on shorts. Then it was back off to Crossroads and then end up in the Horse and Jockey for about five in the morning. This was if we weren't with our girls, but we usually would meet up with them later.

We started the pub crawl usually about 1400hrs until the next morning.

Lumsey and me met his girlfriend and her mate in Traps one night had a few drinks then went off to Crossroads. Lumsey and the girls went up to the bar while I went to the toilet and said "Hello" to my girlfriend working behind the other bar in the corner.

I then noticed a scuffle going on. The Yanks were in again and as I got to the edge of the dancefloor; I could see Charlie having some difficulty with two big black Yanks.

Some new draft who had just arrived from England were just standing there watching. I told them, "Don't just stand there, join in," as I removed my jacket (new) and threw it to my girlfriend.

I then joined Charlie in the arena taking punches and throwing punches, ducking and diving but then I felt a strong blow to my left eye and could feel the blood oozing out. A Yank glass had caught me straight in my face above my eye. I managed to grab hold of the culprit grabbing this big black Yank as blood poured down over my face covering my good looks. I had him in a headlock, but he was pushing me from side to side trying to loosen my grip, grabbing at my legs to pull me to the floor, however I kept him in my grip and notice a few of the lads standing there watching, I pulled the Yank over to them and said, "fucking glass him." Then smack, the Yank was lucky the lad had missed with the glass and hit me slicing open my elbow.

The fight soon stopped and they Yanks went I however had been sliced up, a four-inch slit above my eye and six-inch on my elbow. There was a group of the British nurses standing outside trying to help me but refused to sew me. My girlfriend in a state of shock and Lumsey getting his girls away from the trouble.

So off I went with Charlie who took me back to the sergeant's mess where he cleaned me up before I went to the medical centre and woke up one of my mates who sewed up my elbow but was unable to sew up my face, so I was sent to the British military hospital where I got sown up by the duty doctor, who just happened to be an old rugby colleague. So, he did not report this to the battalion or SIB.

I usually got the worse for wear with beer. On one occasion I drew 150 Hong Kong dollars out of the bank thinking it was 15.

I got a taxi back to the barracks and it came to $4.5 dollars, so I gave the taxi driver $50 thinking it was $5.

The taxi then shot off, wheel spinning, then off it went.

Now the $5 was brown and $50 purple or the other way round so you can see it's an easy mistake. It was about a week later when I realised that I had given the taxi driver a $45 tip. I was in the corporal's mess and ordered a drink I gave him what I thought was $5 and I got change for $50. So being honest I said, "I think you have given me to much change," but he said, "No here's the note I gave you."

I then said, "I will be back in a minute" as I went back to my bunk and there on the cupboard was a nice spanking new $50 note the last of the three. This being a lot of money for a tip back in 1987.

Whilst in Hong Kong I grew up a bit and started treating girls the way they should but had the problem of having more than one girlfriend.

I decided that I had to finish with one of my girlfriends as it was getting too much for me. So one night I had to keep saying to one girl I was with, I will be back in a minute, I've just got to see one of my lads, as I left the pub I was in and went straight across the road to Crossroads to speak to my barmaid girlfriend, then make excuses to her and went back over to the other pub. Then a third girl I was seeing turned up, so I thought enough, enough and finished with one. I have not the brains to keep three girls on the go at one time.

I finished with my barmaid girlfriend. Well, I didn't actually finish with her I got one of the lads in my section to do it for me, as I didn't have the bottle to do this myself.

She was moving to one of the islands in a house where it backed onto the beach. She wanted me to move there with her, but I thought not. Looking back now it would have been a dream move.

My platoon commander had heard all the stories about the Wan Chai and asked me to take him and another officer there before we left Hong Kong, as officers in the Guards were not allowed to associate with commoners like us.

I met up with him and took him and a fellow officer down to Crossroads.

They seemed to be shellshocked with what was going on and only stayed for one drink, thanked me then left. This was all new for them and opened their eyes to what we got up to, a different world for them which they felt uncomfortable with.

One of the other girls I was seeing was a blonde who had the same lovely eyes as Tanya Roberts (James Bond bird, *View to a Kill*), they followed you everywhere.

I stood her up on Christmas day in my second year. Once again, I had not been invited to anyone's house for Christmas, so I went to Ronny Scott's club along with Lumsey his girlfriend and her mate.

My Tanya Roberts was having dinner with her family who didn't approve of squaddies, so I had an enjoyable day on the beer and because I was having such a good time, I stood her up.

She forgave me on Boxing Day, but this may have something to do with her being there when I phoned home only to find out that my dad had died that day. Things as you may imagine weren't the same for me after that for a while.

CHAPTER 6

Holiday

Whilst away in Hong Kong we had two weeks leave in the summer. Some of the lads would return to England and others would try and see parts of South East Asia.

I was all for returning to England but before I left my dad had told me to try and see a bit of the world while I was out here.

I did travel around, and it was some good advice, however it was my dad's last advice to me face to face as he died shortly before my tour of Hong Kong finished.

On my first leave I went on holiday with a lad called Whitey.

Whitey being a big lad, largely built and a head of blond hair. He looked younger than he was, a handsome looking guy.

We went down to the local travel agents and the English woman told us the best place to go and that was the Philippines.

So off we went over the seas to Manila.

We stayed at a place where all the squaddies stayed, called the Kangaroo Club.

We dropped off our bags and went straight on the piss.

Into our first bar, topless women dancing on the tables, women coming straight over to you taking your hands and cutting your nails as a jug of beer was put in front of you.

Then you would receive a massage with the words coming from all of them "You handsome boy, you big and strong." It seemed the woman in the travel agency was right.

We went to a few bars and the woman were all over us and then we met up with a British fellow who took us to his bar gave us free drinks and then two girls.

These are freebies he said to us pointing to the girls.

Whitey and me took these two to a few more bars then straight back to our room where upon we shagged the pair of them silly.

Whitey then caught his trying to steal his wallet, so we booted them both out.

We then went to Angeles City. Stayed in a lovely hotel and again went straight on the piss.

We were walking past these three girls when one says, "You want sample blowjob?"

I said, "Ok then." She said, "Come this way." I said, "No you give me blowjob here." So, she did in the middle of the street.

I had one rubbing my arse while the other gave me head.

I then noticed that the one rubbing my arse was trying to steal my money out my back pocket, so I told them to "Fuck off."

I could not help Whitey though he had gone down the alley with his and one had taken his shorts off while the other gave him head. When he came out, I told him to check his pockets and when he did, he found the bitches had robbed him.

On our first night we went out and tried a few more bars and did some more shagging.

We shagged girls in the shower in the pool and now and again in the bed.

We went to a live sex show one night, it was not too expensive to go in and what a show we had.

There was a woman who would pile up coins and sit on them then spit them from out of her fanny.

We went there the next night too, but we put a lighter to some of the coins and by fuck did she get a shock.

There were also two lesbians having a go at it. There was a woman getting fucked by vibrators another woman shoved her hand and then her arm up to her elbow up this other woman's fanny.

There was another woman being fucked by her mate who was wearing a strap on dildo.

One woman then got my pint and tipped it down her naked body then asked if I wanted my drink. I looked up at her and saw my drink tricking over her small tits, down to her navel and then dripping over her love channel. I nodded my head, yes, I said as she shoved my head straight into her minge and said there you, I think I got every last drop back.

Men were pulled up from the crowd and given free blowjobs and then at the end of the night you could go on the stag and dance with the girls who had just performed this lovely act. Again, back in the 80s as young squaddies, this was something new and a great experience

We started to get to know the security guard well at our hotel and if we had not pulled that night, we would get a knock on the door and he would walk in with about seven woman and we would just pick the one for the night.

One night we went out and got into a fight.

The bar was a sleazy bar, cheap tables and chairs, an old table football machine in one corner. The bar and floor were dirty, an old fan on the wall looking like it was going to fall off and the wind blew the flimsy door, so it kept banging against the doorframe every few seconds.

I had just walked out of the bar with a beer and the bloke on the door grabbed me told me I could not take the bottle with me, so I ignored him and kept going.

He then stopped me and pushed me back inside whereupon the mama-sam said I could not walk off with the beer. I said in England we pay for the bottle as well. She said here the bottle must stay in the bar.

I then accused the bloke saying that I have nicked the beer. She said no he was on about the bottle.

So, I drank up and told her I wanted him to apologise. He would not, so Whitey and I walked out swearing a lot as we walked past him. We went out onto the road and walked past the second door.

The bloke was now at the other door with this big bloke, they stared as us spitting in our direction before they called me a 'wanker'.

I walked over to him and said, "You what," and before I knew it he had smacked me one and put me on my arse. They then came from everywhere.

Whitey was also getting a good kicking as I managed to stand up, but I was soon on my backside again as I was hit over the back with a rifle. I then received a couple of kicks to my body and was then left in a puddle in this road my shoes in another puddle.

Whitey was also in another puddle but we both managed to get up and get our shoes on and started to hobble back to our hotel, with the lads who had just gave us the kicking laughing whilst we hobbled away.

I then stopped and said to Whitey, "Fuck this I'm not taking that," and picked up a bat that I found on the side of the track, Whitey picked up a table and we went back down to this bar again. Our pride had kicked in.

I then shouted, "Come on then let's see what you're made of."

One Filipino came out and said, "You want the same again?" I shouted, "Come on then bring it on." Another lad then came out and shook his head and said, "You're fucking crazy," and walked back inside taking the other chap back inside with him..

Whitey and I sighed a sigh of relief, our pride was intact and went back to the hotel battered and bruised and a little bit lucky.

We went back to Manila for one day and went straight on the piss again.

Whitey left me and took a girl back to the hotel, so I went off down the street on my own. I then heard someone behind me, so I turned around and there stood this tall woman. Dark hair, long wavy dress, a lot of makeup.

"You want fuckie fuckie?" she said. I said, "Wouldn't mind."

She then said, "Where you stay?" I said, "Kangaroo Club."

She then said, "You squaddie?" And I, "Yes."

"I not go with squaddie I am a man," she said.

She then came a little closer, I was looking her/him up and down to see if I could see any signs of a man, she/him then again said I am a man and came nearer to me. So, bang I put her/him/ it on its arse.

The next thing I know is I'm being pulled into his bar by a bloke. "You can't do that son," he said in a broad Scottish accent.

"But that's a fucking bloke," I said. "I know son, most of them are, but you can't go around smacking them all."

I stayed with my new Jock friend then for the rest of the evening after finding out that the bar we were in was his.

The bar was on the right and there were girls dancing on a thin stage behind this.

The place was dark, but I could make out several men sitting along the bar gazing lustfully up at the girls, a beer in front of them and slobber running from the sides of their lips. I was sitting at the end of the bar with my new Jock buddy.

Before long the bar shut, the girls all got off the stage once my Jock buddy had given them the nod. They then got changed and before leaving all gave my new mate a kiss good night.

After they had all gone, we then went through this narrow door into a large room, which was his illegal casino.

He then told me he had to go, told a girl to look after me and drinks were free.

I thanked him and fucked her.

The next day we were flying back to Hong Kong but thought we would go and have a few before we left.

An American had just come into the hotel and asked if he could join us for a drink.

We said OK then and went into the bar. He said he would show us Brits how to drink.

The bar being very bright with a lot of mirrors on the walls and ceilings, very clean, with a lot of girls in bikinis dancing on the stage which was in the middle of the bar and stools going around this.

I then ordered three jugs, and the Yank said you mean one jug, three glasses.

I said no as the three jugs arrived, I then handed one to Whitey and one to the Yank.

Whitey and I downed ours straight away and ordered three more we then knocked these back and got the Yank to get three more. We then knocked these back and then finished of the Yanks two he had not touched yet as he was throwing up in the toilets.

We got to the airport and were steaming and were not allowed onto the plane so slept in the airport for the night and we were put on the first available fight the next day.

In my second year I went to Thailand with a lad called Sav.

Sav was a young lad who had just joined the battalion. A good rugby player and a good lad. I took him under my wing. He was small for the guards, had blond hair and a bulky little body. He did a lot of scrambling on motorbikes at home and was an ace on a motorbike.

We went to Bangkok did a bit of window-shopping (number 17 and number 15 if you know what I mean). Saw some strip shows down Patpong.

We then got on the coach to Pattaya. We travelled to Pattaya drinking all the beer on board and go straight on the piss again.

In every bar we went the girls come up to you again, "Hello handsome." "I love you." "You marry me."

I was not too bothered about shagging because I was in some pain. I thought I had appendicitis and got Sav to take me to this medical centre.

I walked in and Sav said he would pick me up in a bit.

The woman then asked what was the matter with me, so I said I think it is my appendix.

She then tells me to open my mouth and shoves some medicine in my mouth.

I said, "What's that?" "Vitamin C," she said.

She then tells me to take off my clothes, so I do.

Then gives me an injection up my arse. "What's that?" I said. "Vitamin D," she says.

Then she tells me to lie down on this bench and another woman comes in who then gets on top of me and starts to give me a massage.

"You handsome man," she says slapping my arse every now and again.

"You married?" "No," I say without thinking.

"I have a lovely daughter. She very nice. Hard worker. Give you lots of babies."

I now begin to shit myself. Here I am in a foreign country bollock naked, in pain, and have a fat woman sitting on my back telling me to marry her daughter.

"I have a girlfriend," I said.

"No, you meet my daughter. You like her. She still a virgin," said the woman, with the other one agreeing and saying, "I go and get her."

Next thing the door opens, my head now thinking this will be the daughter but as I look around there stands Sav. "You ready yet?" he says.

The woman then gets up tells me I owe her loads of money, so I just grab my clothes push Sav and tell him to leg it.

We then get on Sav's motorbike and shoot of down the main road me still naked.

I did get to an international medical centre who sorted me out.

Sav did plenty of shagging but I stayed off it as I was ill and only stayed a week before going back to South Korea to see an American girlfriend of mine.

CHAPTER 7

South Korea

I went to South Korea on three occasions, twice with the United Nations and once on holiday.

I was the only one in the battalion to do the two tours in Korea with the United Nations.

We were stopping in the American garrison barracks, which were more like a little town.

There were supermarkets, three nightclubs, car showrooms, cinemas, sport pitches, about 12 baseball pitches, barber shops, the place had everything.

There were about 1000 Yanks to each of us.

We were there as part of the honour guard and we had to do guard duty on the four-star general's house as well as ceremonial parades.

We all had to learn the American drill.

We arrived in Seoul and went straight to the barracks and then into our block.

The honour guard would be made up from the Yanks, Koreans, Thailand soldiers, Filipino soldiers, and us.

We met up with the American captain who told us what was expected from us all.

They were a bit worried about us because the last time there was a Guard's regiment out there, they had trouble with them.

This was the Scots Guards who were supposed to have put a bike up the flagpole and painted pink spots on the Yank tanks.

We got on with the Yanks in the honour guard and they all wanted to buy our Union Jack shorts off us and couldn't believe we wore these, as they never put their flag on the ground.

We found this out once while rehearsing for a flag parade.

They had these massive flags that needed three strong men to carry.

The Yanks would bring theirs out and place it on two chairs; the Koreans did the same.

We came out with the United Nations flag threw it on the grass bank and lay down, using it as a massive pillow.

This was only until the Yank captain saw it and threw a fit.

We did a lot of running with the Yanks. With them singing as they ran.

They then asked us to do a song, so as we were running through the married quarters, we all start to sing.

"I gave her inches one, the stories just began, roll me over lay me down and do it again, roll me over in the clover roll me over lay me down and do it again."

The Yanks thought this was good until we got to the fifth and sixth verse.

"I gave her inches five, the spunk began to rise, roll me over lay me down and do it again."

"I gave her inches six, the spunk began to mix."

They then realised what we were on about and shouted you cannot sing that and in the end the Yanks did the singing.

We also did some live firing with the Yanks, but we beat them on the ranges with their weapons the M16s and we also beat them when we put the grenade launchers on the weapons (M16 203).

We were supposed to all go on exercise as well but it rained so the Yanks cried off, but we still went.

Now on the piss was brilliant, there were bars everywhere and we could do what we wished.

The bars were on every corner and it was much better than in Hong Kong.

We went to the place where the main bars were and went to a few before going up this hill.

On both sides of this hill there were women. "Hey Mister, you want fuckie, fuckie?" was all we got.

These women were nice, and we asked the Yanks about them. The Yanks said that's Hooker's Hill and they are all hookers.

So, when we went back down the hill we would go over to them and get a good feel.

The hookers thought they had some randy soldiers for a change instead of the Yanks who would stand there not touching like gentleman discussing a price.

We got our free feels for about a week telling the hookers we would be back later, but they soon caught on that we were just getting a handful now and again as none of us Brits had yet shagged one of them.

We then would walk up Hooker's Hill and they would stand against the wall and spit at us saying, "Fucking British, no good fuckie fuckie, you number 10."

The mama-sam would ask us "You want young girl?" What age? I get for you. Or you want boy? I get for you." We couldn't believe this was allowed to happen.

I met up with some British topless dancers in the Kings Club one night.

The Kings Club being one of the main places. It was big, you would go in turn left and the bar would be over on the left going along the full length of the club and finishing up just before the small dancefloor.

Between the bar and the opposite wall were tables and chairs.

In one bit you would have the black Yanks in another you would have the Puerto Ricans and then there were the white Yanks here and there. There were Korean women on every table being chatted up. The music being loud, as you would expect and the disco lights flashing around.

The topless dancing girls were right stuck-up bitches who moaned that they had come all the way to Korea only to be chatted up by some Brits.

They could not have been that bothered as I shagged one of them that night.

They were leaving in a week's time and told us that a new troop would be taking over from them.

The new troop came, and I had been waiting for them to arrive and watching for new faces in the Kings Club. I then noticed some new pretty faces and pounced before the Yanks had a chance.

The girls were really glad to meet some British lads and hated the Yanks.

That night I went back with them to their hotel.

I was with one of the girls but fancied another and the feeling was the same.

To my surprise the one I was with and the one I fancied shared the same bed, so I jumped in between them both.

I then shagged/made love to the one I was supposed to be with while the one I fancied pretended to be asleep.

I did not last that long as I was pissed and all three of us fell asleep.

In the early hours I woke and was pretty rampant, so I looked over to the girl I had shagged already. She was fast asleep, so I turned over to the other girl who was also awake and gave me a little smile.

I then let my finger do the walking again whilst swapping some spit.

We then got up and went out onto the balcony where I then took her standing up from behind, we then returned to bed and in the morning I said I would get turned on if they both played with each other, so after a while of them thinking about it with me urging them on, they said fuck it we might as well.

I think they had done this before, but I watched as they both started to tongue wrestle and play with each other's breasts.

They then got all shy on me and stopped but invited me to once again lie in between them, which I did willingly. One started to kiss me while the other went down on me.

We then did a few other things, but this soon became too much for me and I shot my load.

I started seeing the girls on a regular basis whilst in Korea and kept in touch with them throughout the rest of my army career. One of them actually asked me to marry her at a later date (mad bitch).

The first tour of Korea was good, and we only got into about four fights between us.

One of those was when we walked into a bar and a Yank thought he was Rambo but this was not the case and we gave it him and his Yank friends.

The next night we had been told that these Yanks would be coming down the Kings Club with a number of friends.

We went down the club and stood the length of the bar waiting for these Yanks to show.

Some black Yanks (built like brick shithouses) came over to us and said that if we were having any trouble with the white Yanks then they would be on our side.

The white Yanks did not show, we took over the dancefloor with the Union Jack flying above our heads. The black Yanks just loved us.

We all had to go for dose checks on a regular basis. On one occasion, Orville went for his.

He was gone for most of the day, so I went to see where he had got to.

I noticed him hobbling back to the rooms and asked if he was ok.

He said no the bastards have circumcised me.

He had only gone for a check-up and they had made him an honorary Jew.

We got back into our room and he asked me if I was a good mate.

I said of course I am we have been through a lot together and have been mates for years.

He said good because I need my dressing changed each day and my cock washed in salt water.

I said you can fuck off, I'm not touching your cock.

But you're my mate, I can't do it, I need help, he said.

Right, I said wait here, returning with a new draft under my arm.

I told him what he had to do, he said he wouldn't, but he did and I just hope Orville thanked him.

I had pissed Orville off before this by doing the same thing to him as I had done to Thorn in the Falklands.

I wrote a letter to him from his girlfriend in England (he was no longer a virgin soldier) saying once again that she had found someone else and that his sister had seen her with him. She wanted to own up before his sister told him.

I said in the letter the normal things like "I love you but am not in love with you," and "I want us to remain friends."

Orville had just paid for a ticket to return home and was going to get engaged to her.

He got the letter on mail call and lay on his bed to read this. I asked whom it was from? And he said it was from his mum.

After about five minutes he threw the letter on the floor and started shouting "Fucking bitch, I've just got a Dear John." I said, "What from your mum?"

"No, from my girlfriend, here read it," as he picked up the letter and passed it to me, not knowing that I knew what was in the letter.

I pretended to read it and then tried to console my mate.

I didn't tell him for about two days, but the lads and I said we would tell him before our football match that we had with the Yanks, as Orville was in goal for us.

I had made up the name of the bloke his girlfriend was supposed to be with, but Orville said the worst thing about it all was that he knew this bloke.

We told Orville before the game that I had wrote the letter, but he didn't believe us but thanked us for pretending and trying to make him feel better. He said he knew it was from her.

He would not believe us until he received a letter from her.

However, when he went home on leave, he ended finishing with her because he said he could not trust her.

You could take females back to your room over here in Korea and with my dancing girls away I went out and got off with this Korean girl. A nice little pretty thing.

I took her back to my room and we shagged in every position imaginable.

I was fucking good if I say so myself (my Aussie bird would have been proud) and was fucking for a long time and could not come.

She then got the pillowcase and started wiping herself.

I thought, you know you have had a good shagging don't you babe? I thought she must be coming like Victoria Falls.

There then was a bang on the door. "What's the door locked for?" It was Orville again, just returned from town and he had not pulled.

Let us have a go he said. (His cock must have been feeling better.)

I said help yourself and then asked her if Orville could shag her.

She said no and asked if she could have a shower.

I said no as the showers were shared and not on their own, she got her clothes on and fucked off.

I then told Orville of my last two hours of shagging as you do.

I then said, "Yeah I gave her a right good fucking she had to get the pillow and wipe herself." I then reached for the pillow which was under the bed.

Orville started to laugh his fucking head off as I looked down at the pillow and seeing it was no longer my brilliant white pillowcase, but now scarlet red covered in blood.

I then looked at my fingers they were also covered in blood, as was my cock and when I investigated in the mirror so was my face.

I quickly jumped into the shower and Orville could not wait to tell the lads.

Not long after I got off with this really tasty Korean. She seemed different from the others, very pretty and a perfect body.

I took her back to the barracks but did not realise that you had to be in the barracks before 12 if you wanted to take a girl back.

She then said to me, "You say I can come back, it's ok."

I then said, "I got in here before with a girl."

"You bring girl here before?" she says

"No," I said (quick thinking). "My mate brought a girl back here before, I'm a virgin"

"You no virgin," she said, "you no cherry boy."

"Yes, I'm a cherry boy, honest," I said.

I did not know that it was a big thing out there for a girl to take your cherry.

She then said, "Why you want me to take your cherry?"

I said, "I think you are a lovely girl, I couldn't wish for anyone better than you to take my cherry."

Next thing you know she said we go back to my house.

I thought she meant her house but as we walked in there was mum, dad, brothers, sisters, nan, granddad and an auntie.

She then started talking to them in Korean, with me just standing there smiling at them all, nodding my head as to say hello, then she asks me to follow her taking me upstairs.

She then made love to me, starting with soft kisses from head to toe, followed by a nice blowjob before taking the leading role as I pretended to be her little cherry boy.

Latter we went downstairs, her little sisters started to giggle as her dad came over to me shook my hand and hugged me.

The mother came over with some shitty, cheap wine and we all had that.

I think they thought this was going to be their daughter's future husband.

I said I would see her the next night and left.

I told all the lads what had happened and the next night they were all down the town telling all the Korean girls they were cherry boys.

Also in the barracks was a steam room where you could go and have a bath and massage.

We called this the steam and cream.

You would go up have a bath and then they would ask you if you wanted any extras.

The answer was always yes, and you would get a nice Thomas the Tank off them.

This was unbelievably cheap as well.

The night before we left, I had asked my topless dancing girlfriend if we could come and watch them at their show.

At this time, the girls hadn't told us they were topless dancers, even though we already knew.

My girl said ok, but I had to come on my own. She gave me the address of the hotel where they were performing.

I then turned up with all the lads and we were sat at the back. The waiter told us we had to pay for the table, but I told him they were my girlfriends and he let us off.

The show started and the girls came out with their tits out.

We made the most noise and when I spoke to her later, she said she couldn't see at the back because of the lights, but she could here loads of shouting and people shouting for the girls to get all their kit off. She said you were on your own weren't you, and of course I said I was.

One of the Yank corporals was a right arsehole and before we left, I ordered eight whopping big pizzas and 20 Dr Pepper drinks, 20 French fries and garlic bread saying I was Corporal Beard and I was ordering them as it was one of the honour guards birthdays.

We boarded the coach for the airport and were waved off by our Yank friends.

No pizza.

We then drove around to the front and there was this pizza deliveryman struggling up the stairs with these pizzas and drinks. The coach just erupted into laughter.

I went back to Korea the second year. I helped to teach the new British honour guard the American arms drill and then we were off to Korea.

As I had already been there, I told all the lads how good it was on the piss and we had all decided to go on the piss straight away.

We got to the honour guard. I met up with a few of my old Yank friends but most of the honour guard had changed.

The new captain then gave us the welcome speech and then our sergeant major gave us a talking to.

He said he knew that I had told everyone about how good it was on the piss but suggested that we get our rooms sorted out first as we had ten weeks to see the nightlife.

This was good advice from the sergeant major who was a right hard nut who said I reminded him of himself in his younger days.

He was still a skinhead, was very muscular and just looked tough, very patriotic, nobody would mess with him and he had the respect from all of us.

Whilst in Korea he had a Union Jack suit made for him. Something that I also had made some many years later.

The lads then all said that the sergeant major was right, and they had all decided to stay in.

I told the sergeant major that I was still going out and he said he thought as much anyway.

I then went from one room to the other saying that the other lads are coming out aren't you lot? They said, well if the others are going out then they would.

It was then into another room using the same routine.

I then got changed, walked out the door and the sergeant major was looking out of his window.

He shouted over to me to behave tonight. I said I would, and I would look after the rest, as the rest of the lads then came out of the door behind me like a flock of geese.

It was off up to Hooker's Hill again, into the bars and saying hello to the Korean bar staff I had met the year before.

The year before we had only got into four fights between us all. This time I had 14 fights myself.

One night I was in a bar by myself with my Yank girlfriend. This Yank walked in picked up a chair and stood in front of me. I stood up and asked if there was any problem.

The Yank said, yeah man you, I don't like you Brits, and then came at me, rather aggressively.

I hit him twice, the first being a right punch to the left side of his face, followed by an upper cut sending him on his arse and then walked out with my girlfriend.

However, his two watching mates then grabbed my arms as he got up and again came over to me.

He thought himself safe with his mates now holding onto me and got right in my face saying again what he thought of the Brits.

With both my arms held down I pulled my head back and smashed him on the bridge of his nose sending him toppling back his nose moving across his face and blood pouring from it.

He was dazed and could not get up. I shook his mates off me, I could tell there were not interested in fighting me and said don't fuck with the Brits before leaving with my girl hurrying down Hooker's Hill and meeting up with the rest of the lads in the Kings Club.

One of our lads was a virgin so we took him to Hooker's Hill, all chipped in and sent him off with a hooker. He was really up for this with a broad grin coming over his face.

He came back about 20 minutes later, and the grin had gone and said it was shit, is that all there is to it? He did not know what all the fuss was about when it came to shagging.

Two weeks on our regular dose check, he found out that the whore had only given him a dose.

I had made friends with one of the Yanks in the honour guard. He was a right big lad, well over 6ft6 and was called 'Meat'. No doubt meaning his manhood was also a big boy.

We got into a fight one night and he only went and hit one of the Yank sergeants in the honour guard who did not like him and ended up being arrested.

I stuck up for him and was interviewed all the way up until we left.

The sergeant tried to get me arrested as well but I was the equivalent rank as him and told him where to go.

Meat was not allowed out whilst we remained in Korea even though I had a running battle with their captain as he was being made a scapegoat.

I did manage to get him out to play rugby for us on a couple of occasions. He thanked me for getting him out of camp, but rugby was a bit much for the Yanks, no headgear or padding they kept saying.

On one of the parades the Yanks gave their usual speil about what a strong country they were and how the Koreans were there best allies and had always been and both countries had a bright future together. This however did not go down well with us and caused a bit of shit and we fell out with a lot of them over this.

The sergeant major even contemplated marching us off the parade.

A lot of the Yanks thought we were special forces as we wore berets and only the Yank special forces wear these. So we were always getting saluted, and this is probably why they let us get away with so much downtown.

We played the Yanks at rugby and won, American football and won and baseball and won.

We were supposed to be playing rugby before a big parade, but the honour guard captain would not allow this as he said there would be to many injures so we played baseball.

I split someone's head open when I hit a good ball and just tossed the bat behind me. Another lad broke his leg; one sprained his hand and another his ankle. No such injuries in rugby.

We travelled around and we were sent to the DMZ (demilitarized zone) where we had to bury the first North Korean bodies on South Korean soil since the war.

This was a big parade which made the news on most television channels.

Back down the town and again I got into a right big fight.

We called this bloke 'Sting', because he looked like Sting, the singer from The Police. With his thin look but bleached blond/white hair.

I was in the Kings club one night when two of the younger lads came into me and said this Yank had just given them a good hiding, one of the lads being Sav.

I told them to show me this lad and we walked out down the road and past Hooker's Hill there was Sting bragging to his mates on what he had just done.

I told the lads to get into him, which they did. Which resulted in Sting being left in a heap on the floor, no longer bragging. I did not get involved and just watched. After it had finished, I sent both lads back to the barracks to get cleaned up a bit, as they were both in a state. Having fat lips and cuts around their faces, eyes beginning to swell up, I then returned to Kings Club and met up with the rest of the lads.

About ten minutes later in walks a Yank who asks one of our lads, which Brit is in charge?

The lad pointed to me and the Yank asked me the same. I looked around and was the senior one there so said I suppose I am, and he said my mate wants a word with one of you outside.

I went outside with the rest of the lads following in tow and there was Sting standing in the middle of the road. Looking not so smart now,

So, I went over to him and he just said he wanted to fight one of the two lads that had just given him a kicking down the road.

I said they were only young lads and he and his mates had earlier given them a good kicking, so why not just leave it, trying to be diplomatic.

He said he did not care and wanted me to get them back, which I refused. He said he wanted to fight one of them. I said just leave it now both parties had given and received a few punches, so let us leave it and have a few beers instead,

I said that I had sent them back to the barracks to get cleaned up.

He then said ok I will fight another Brit.

So, I said if he wanted to fight another Brit then it would have to be me. Hoping he would turn down my generous offer.

The wind seemed to have stopped and the sky was clear.

I did not know at this time, but a big crowd had gathered and made an oval shape around us, the traffic in the road had come to a standstill and the bars were pulling down the shutters.

Sting then said ok I will fight you down that alley. Pointing to an alley across the road.

I said if he wanted to fight me then it would have to be here and now.

He was trying to wind me up and goad me, but I kept giving him smart answers and not getting dragged in.

He then said that he was an Irish-American.

I said bully for you I don't give a shit.

He then said he supported the IRA – again I said I don't give a shit, smiling at him.

We had all had these T-shirts made for us and on the front of them in bright red it said QUEENS GUARDS.

Sting then looked at my shirt and said the queen's a slag.

I then heard Phil a fellow corporal that I was sharing a room with say to this bird, "Oh shit, watch this."

I asked Sting what he had said again, and he replied, "The Queen's a slag."

I then pulled back my head like pulling back the bolt on the old rifle and then released the trigger and before Sting knew it, I had smashed my forehead against his nose breaking it and sending blood pouring from it.

I then followed this up with a few punches, but he had somehow rugby tackled me.

I was still standing but my punches would not connect where I wanted them to go, as his head was low. He was moving his head from side to side whilst trying to grapple with me.

I then tried to boot him but once again could not.

We fell against a car and I somehow managed to grab head smashing it against the car.

He was pushing me up along the car, as I was still smashing his head on it and we came to the aerial that was sticking up about an inch. I smashed his head against this and then we were up to another car. The cars changing colour with the red blood leaving a nice mess on both cars.

I pulled his head up and saw a mass of blood, you could not see his smashed nose or recognise his face.

I pulled by my right arm and punched him in the face for the last time just as two big black Yanks came running over, grabbing me, and pulling me away from Sting who had now just dropped to the floor in a heap, a broken man.

The two big black dudes said he has had enough. Phil then joined me as I turned to the two black lads, adrenaline running high, asking if they also wanted some.

They said, look man just leave it now, go please go.

I was then pulled under these shutters by another Yank. I stood up said you want some?

My adrenaline still doing overtime.

He said, "No man I'm on your side," and pointed to the two vans of riot police that had just turned up.

We were back in Kings Club and I was calming down, Yanks were walking up to me shaking my hand.

"You Brits are brilliant," they were saying. "Someone slags off your queen and you give it them, fucking brilliant."

Another Yank said every time I see one of you Brits I'm going to buy you a drink. (We always somehow managed to find him after this.)

A Puerto Rican big friend of mine kept moving his head forward and asking me what's that called it's brilliant.

Sting got stung and we did not see him again.

On one night I got into an argument with my American girlfriend, she went off home in a mood, so I just stayed in this bar and got myself pissed.

I then left the bar and walked down Hooker's Hill.

I then met a whore who asked me if I wanted anything.

I thought fuck it, I will get myself a blowjob.

I then said, how much for a blowjob.

She then gave me a good price and liking a bargain said ok, but you do it here down the alleyway.

The next thing I know I'm naked on her bed she puts some porn on TV and says she will be back in a minute.

She then returns in leather and telling me she wants to tie me up.

I said no way I just want head. She then sits on me and starts to bite into my chest.

This fucking hurts but I just grit my teeth and take it.

She then starts on my stomach, again this hurting, and then she takes one of my bollocks into her mouth and starts sucking.

This was a better feeling until she decides to sink her teeth into this as well.

I suddenly shoot up. "That fucking hurt," I say as my eyes start to fill up.

She pushes me back down and starts to suck my cock. It was then back to my bollocks and again she sinks her teeth into it.

I soon sobered up, that is it I say I can't take anymore as I get up and start to dress.

I then pay her and return to the barracks.

The next day I was having a shower and one of the lads says you been with Kinky?

I said yea how do you know.

He then shows me his chest, which was covered in bite bruises.

There were five of us who went through this agony with her.

I made up with my girlfriend but kept my shirt on for a while.

Before we left Korea, the four-star general said to us that if any of us ever returned to Korea then they would put us up.

But they never kept their word because I popped back to see my American girlfriend and their captain would not put me up. He said if it were anyone else then yes, but for me it was a big no as, he thought I would be too much trouble. WHY??

My American girlfriend's father (a two-star general) didn't like me, but her mother did like me, so they had arguments as to where I would stay, and in the end the father won, and I ended up stopping in a shitty hotel where Yanks would take whores to shag them.

I left Korea after a week my girlfriend was sent back to the states and that was that.

CHAPTER 8

Up Above The Clouds

The last place I went to before leaving South East Asia was to Brunei on the island of Borneo.

This was on an expedition and there would be 12 of us picked for it.

The last part of the expedition was to enter the thick jungle and navigate our way to a waterfall, when we had completed this we had to set up camp and then spend a couple of days chopping down trees and vines to make a ladder at the side of the waterfall. The first part would be to build a raft again from the trees and vines and then travel down Belait River, with the second part we had to travel to Malaysia and climb Mount Kinabalu.

So off we went to complete the first part of the expedition and we all went down to this river where we set up camp and spent two days building this raft.

There had been warning in the papers that week that a lot of crocodiles had been seen in the river just lately and the officials had advised everyone to stay out of the river.

A lot of people used the river for water skiing.

But we ignored this advice as we were squaddies

We entered part of the jungle and cut trees down using our machetes, different size trees and branches. Once we had built the raft, we all stood back, after a lot of planning and building and arguing, we managed to build our raft and had a look at our hard work.

Masterpiece, maritime revaluation, should carry us all, unsinkable, all the comments now coming from all of us dockers. We had worked out that it should carry five of us with the rest in the safety boat.

It was then the time for its maiden voyage, we didn't have any champagne to launch it with, so we just pushed it into the river and…

Like its sister ship the *Titanic* it sank but not after half of her journey, not hitting an iceberg (far too hot for one of these). It just sank.

Well, not completely. It still floated but a layer of water would just cover it.

We then knew it would not take us all or even five, so we had a democratic vote to see who would test this out.

The new draft.

We all said it had to be the sprog of the group to try this out.

"But there's fucking crocodiles in that river," he said.

"You'll be ok, we will watch out for them while we pull you along in the boat."

The new draft then got on the raft as we pulled him out into the heart of the river, which was like tar, you could not see anything.

We pulled him behind us for several miles down the river.

He was glued to the small mast that we had built, the river coming over his feet as the raft just stayed afloat, his eyes going from left to right checking both banks. Then looking around the sides of the raft before checking both banks again. He would then look at us with despair in his eyes looking for somebody anybody to come to his aid and show some compassion, of course this did not happen from any of us who were sat safely on the safety boat.

We then came to a clearing where we said we would set up camp, so we pulled over to the bank, pulled the raft onto the bank as the relieved new draft jumped off onto land and ran straight behind a bush and emptied himself.

We then made camp, got some wood and made a fire.

Some of the lads made up the bashers while others got wood and I cooked dinner with the help from some of the others.

After we had eaten and the night came in, we sat around the fire telling jokes, stories etc.

'Step', our sergeant, decided it was time for bed and had set up his basher away from everybody else.

I had decided that I would be sleeping in between two of the lads because if any crocodiles did want an early breakfast then it would be them first before me.

Step then went to bed, but before he did, he went around his basher clearing all the leaves away and then making a circle around his basher with insect repellent.

We all took the piss, but he went off to sleep.

Before we all got our heads down, we swept away the insect repellent and replaced this with sugar and bits of food.

In the morning Step woke complaining that the insect repellent was shit and he had been bitten to fuck during the night and could not get a good night's sleep. We all slept well as the insects were too busy with Step and crocodiles had left us alone.

We packed up camp and went off down the river again, this time pulling someone else behind us.

Another couple of miles and one of the lads said, "Fuck it I'm going in," and dived into the river and swam over to the raft.

We then said fuck the crocodiles, let's all get in, and we all did except for Step.

We all got onto the raft, but I must admit I was shitting myself as I swam from the boat to the raft, as you couldn't see anything beneath you.

I got to the raft and we all started fighting to get the best, safest or most secure spot.

I think I got this as I now became glued to the mast, only my feet moving to kick anyone off who got too near to me.

The person in charge was an officer who we will call by his first name, 'Rupert'.

Rupert was my platoon commander, so I knew him very well and as Guard's officers went, he was a great bloke.

The Guard's officers are usually from the upper class and treated you as just commoners, but Rupert did not, and I respected him for this and for his man management.

After the expedition he told me he was going to organise another one to the Himalayas and asked if I would go with him again? Of course, I said yes but I got out of the army before he organised this.

Rupert joined us in the river and like I said it was only Step who shit himself and would not join us.

We got to the pickup point and did not come across any crocodiles. They must have been told there were some mad squaddies around and thought better of meeting up with us.

Next part of the expedition was to travel down river after river across part of a sea in these boats that were more like canal barges and go into Malaysia.

Once there we hired a minibus that was like cramming sardines into a can and travelled in sweltering heat down track after track until we got to Mount Kinabalu, which is the highest mountain in South East Asia at 13,455 feet.

We spent that night getting ready for the next day before going on the piss again.

The next day we split up into three groups, fast, slow, and even slower.

I oversaw the fast group and only had three others in this group with me.

We put our mountain climbing boots on, packed our rucksacks and off we went.

At 11,000 feet there was some accommodation, which we would sleep in that night before making the climb to the peak the next morning (which we would be doing together).

My group got to 11,000 feet, found out which was our accommodation and then made up our bunks and got the food on for the others and a hot drink.

The next group arrived an hour later. We helped them in and gave them the hot drinks they were dying for.

The last group got to us about another 30 minutes later.

That night we had some beers and, because of the altitude, we lost half the can when opening them.

The lads all went to bed then, but I noticed two Malaysian girl climbers making some tea, so I was straight over to them and started chatting them up.

All the lads could hear this and I was soon joined by another two lads.

I thought here I go, I'm going to join the 11,000ft high club as I thought the girls liked me.

But then two big Malaysian mountaineering blokes appeared from their rooms, came across to the girls and asked if their tea was ready which they said nearly.

The girls then introduced us to their boyfriends who shook our hands and invited us to join them for their meal.

I said no thanks and went off to my bunk wishing they had asked me to share their women instead.

The next morning, we went with the guide to the peak, looked at the scenery and took loads of photographs. We then spent the rest of the morning doing some abseiling before returning to the base of the mountain and then over the next day back to Brunei.

Our final part of the expedition was to go into the jungle and find this waterfall and make a ladder.

There had been a plane that had come down in the jungle a lot of years before but every time parties were sent to try and find it they could never find it.

One of our companies the year before tried but could not find it.

The amazing thing was a lot of people had just stumbled on it, logged it down on the map, but could never find it again.

But this did not bother us because we did not find it either.

We got to the waterfall, which we did find; set up base camp and all dived or jumped off the fall, except for Step again. Most of us coming out with leeches stuck to us.

We grabbed Rupert and tossed him off the top in a leg and a wing.

We made the ladder chopping down the tallest trees and putting it together.

A group of tourists with a guide came along and watched. At this point I was checking out these girls, showing off my Rambo skills, when, 'swish', I had only just put a machete into my hand blood pouring everywhere.

The women in the tourist party saw this and started screaming, I looked down and then I just got up, put one of my smelly socks around the gaping wound, and walked back to the base camp.

As I walked past the group of tourists, I said don't worry about it, I've got another hand.

I went back to base camp and Rupert said he would call for a helicopter and get me casevac'ed. Even though a nice helicopter ride would have been nice I said I would be ok as one of the lads put some butterfly stitches in for me.

We had a few beers that night, tried to get some sleep but all you could hear was the monkeys having fun and making very strange noises throughout the night, and then in the morning massive hornets trying to get into our bashers and through our mosquito nets. When we got up, we lowered the ladder over the fall.

Only about four lads climbed the ladder before it fell. We did manage to erect it again, but it fell again and smashed up. Well, that is us, we are infantry and not carpenters or the pioneer core.

We returned to the Gurkhas barracks where upon the medical staff would not sew up my hand as it was over 24 hours and it needed stitching before that. (It did get stitched about a week later when I opened it up again in a rugby match in Hong Kong.)

We then went out for a meal in Brunei and found where they served beer.

On the way back to the barracks I noticed two girls across a road that called to us.

I went over to the girls with one of the lads in my section, Lardie.

We quickly chatted them up and the girls asked us to follow them, so off we went down this log road and into an empty house.

Lardie being smaller than me with dark hair a little bit tubby had got off with the best one and I thought, "Shall I pull rank?" but in the end I thought I would leave it.

The one I was with was a right ugly fucker so I thought I'm not going to shag it; I will just get a blowjob.

Lardie had gone into a separate room with his and I stayed with mine.

We were both pissed so I told mine I just wanted a blowjob.

No, I am a man was the reply I got. Fuck off, I said show us your cock then.

No, you show me yours it said. It was not going to be déjà vu from Manila,

I then got my cock out and showed it.

I then said get yours out then.

Again, the reply was no, so I thought fuck it I will have head any way because I'm pissed.

I said just give me head.

Again, it said no I'm a man, show us your cock then I said.

And then he pulled out his cock.

I was just about to smack him then I remember smacking the one in the Philippines and as I wasn't too sure of the laws out here, so I just let him/her go.

I then went into the room where Lardie was and saw him in the corner with his, swapping spit and playing with his/her tonsils. I then thought fuck it I will leave him while he is enjoying himself.

I then started walking back down this road and about five minutes later, there was Lardie running up the road behind me. They are blokes, he shouted; they are fucking blokes.

I know I said. I saw you enjoying yourself so I thought I would leave you.

You bastard he said and then he would not tell me how he found out.

We left the next day and returned to Hong Kong.

Did not get into a fight, not even with a crocodile.

CHAPTER 9

The Wart

A lot of squaddies end up with a dose whether it be NSU, crabs or Aids.

We all had lessons on safe sex but there was always a big queue on sick parade for the dose clinic.

When I first joined the battalion and one of the lads had a genital wart, I thought how disgusting this was, and when Ted got crabs I thought he was a dirty bastard.

We had regular dose checks whilst away.

Well, I could not believe it when I was giving my cock its daily inspection and looked down and saw this little wart coming out of my jap's eye.

It cannot be, I thought, not me as I tried to rub it away and found that it wouldn't go.

Well, I'm not keeping this fucker even if it gives better friction.

As I was in Hong Kong I went off to the British military hospital, whereupon I was given the normal test.

Blood taken, a sample placed on slide, another on another slide and then I was told to put a urine sample in the jar on the shelf.

I looked down and then up and then I said what from here. Very funny said the doctor as he handed me the jar.

I then had the umbrella shoved down my jap's eye and then pulled out again.

The doctor then confirmed yes that is a genital wart.

Oh, fuck is there any way you can get rid of it? Yes, we have this acid paint that I will paint on for you which will burn the wart off, he said.

I then held open my jap's eye as this acid was painted on. It was a little painful, but not too bad.

The wart was supposed to drop off in a week but did not, so I was off down to the hospital every month for this paint to be put on. The wart did go but kept coming back so this went on for about a year.

The doctor then said as it had been going on for a while, he would now try some sulfuric acid on it and said this would get rid of it. This stuff would freeze it off.

He then said, I would rather you lie down as you're a big lad and I don't fancy you fainting on me. I said I will not faint, but the doctor said bigger blokes than you have fainted before.

I then lay down, my trousers and boxer shorts at my ankles. The doctor then put his gloves on and brought this blue canister out. He then opened the top of this and there was a cloud of freezing smoke that came from this.

He then made me promise that I would not hit him, which of course I did.

He said this would be very painful and asked me once again to open my jap's eye as he put this acid on the wart.

This did not hurt even though I thought it would.

I was over the moon a couple of weeks later when the wart was gone and thought that was the end of my little friend.

But whilst in Northern Ireland my little friend reappeared so once again, I was off to the clinic and the acid to burn this off was applied again.

My friend stayed with me until I returned to England and I was then sent off to Woolwich hospital, where I had all the tests again and then a nurse took me into a cubicle and interviewed me asking what treatment I had already received and then told me that they were going to give me the electric shock treatment.

She then told me it would be very painful, I said yea, they said that about the sulfuric acid and that did not hurt.

I was then taken into the surgery where I was laid on the bed my trousers and boxer shorts down to my knees, a blanket put across me.

The nurse said she would be with me throughout this.

The doctor then walked in and went through what was going to happen. He then said this is the sound you will here as he squeezed the trigger of the tool that he had in his hand.

The nurse then grabbed my hand and said she would hold this.

I said there was no need as I can take pain.

The doctor then picked up the tool, I heard the noise and thought "That don't fucking hurt," but I didn't know it was the doctor just testing this tool. He then placed it into my jap's eye and the pain just hit me. I grabbed the nurse's hand and squeezed like hell, my teeth were clenched together, and it was going through my head the pain will stop it will stop and then it did.

My grip eased from the nurse's hand and I opened my mouth to take in some breaths as the sweat ran down my face. I thought it was all over, but it all started again.

I again grabbed the nurse's hand and tried to take this unbearable pain but it soon became unbearable as I let go of her hand, my legs shooting up and my hand knocking the tool out of the doctors hand sending it flying across the room and me shouting fuck it leave it I can't take anymore I will keep the wart I'm not going through that again.

The wart went but once again reappeared so this time I went to a civvy hospital who gave me the same treatment, but this time put me to sleep and my friend has never come back to see me, thank fuck.

I remember one bloke who had been away on exercise and had been shagging it around. He thought he had got a dose and knew his wife would want sex with him when he returned. He asked us all to help him with a good excuse but knew she would not wear any of them, so in the end thought it was best just to own up and say it was just a one off silly drunken one-night stand.

He returned from exercise and owned up. She went mad, punched, and kicked the shit out of him and then went of downtown to get her own back.

He then went to the dose clinic and got a check-up, a week later he got his results and got all clear.

Who says honesty always pays?

Four lads in one of the platoons were coming to the end of the tour in Hong Kong and all chipped in to buy this rubber doll.

They then drew up a rota and took it in turns what nights they were having her.

This all became the laugh on the morning parades we all wanted to know who she spent the night with, and did she take a threesome.

But in the end one of the lads got too possessive with her and would not share her, locking himself in his room as the lads outside listened to his grunts and groans.

It was probably the first time he had been steady.

The bloke was that obsessed with it that he ended up showering with it and rubbing his turds on her arse to make it seem more lifelike.

The lads who were sharing it with him soon got bored as they only did it for a laugh but could not believe how jealous he had got so one night they stuck a pin in her and popped it and the lad was devastated spent a couple of nights in tears but managed to get over this tragic loss.

One of the lads who had been with it after the others swears it was the rubber doll that had given him a dose.

CHAPTER 10

Home Sweet Home

We all returned to England and moved into our new barracks in London. We sorted out our kit and then it was off on leave.

For me this was the first leave that I had in England for two years. So off I went home, getting changed and off out on the piss to see my mates.

After a thoroughly enjoyable leave it was back to barracks and back into work.

Hong Kong was an absolutely brilliant place but there's nothing like coming home to England, it's the best place in the world, its weather and everything.

We went from going out on the piss in the Wan Chai to going out on the piss down the West End or wherever took our fancy in London.

We went to most of the London nightclubs but usually were turned away or got barred from the top ones.

But soon knew which ones we could get in and could not.

I was once in the Hippodrome and pissed out of my head a young lady had been singing and then went around on the stage talking to some people. She would ask you your name and where you came from and things like that.

She picked me out of the crowd and said you are a handsome looking bloke and what is your name? I think she regretted this straightaway as I played up to the crowd everyone started laughing, she was trying to get the microphone from me, but I wasn't letting go. This was only until I saw three big bouncers hurrying over to where I was.

I then climbed on the stage slipping over twice as the bouncers also jumped on the stage chasing me across it.

I somehow managed to get away from them and no punches had been thrown. I managed to get up some stairs with the three bouncers following me and then I saw two more coming at me on the floor that I was on.

I looked over the balcony and saw everyone in the club looking up at me, my mates shouting for me to keep going.

I thought about jumping over the balcony into the crowd, but I knew that this wasn't going to be the great escape, so as Steve McQueen did. I stopped held up my hands and let the bouncers escort me from there club.

The crowd loved it and I was cheered all the way to the doors.

Another place we would go to was a place called The Café de Paris I think. Which was more for the older people, a pianist playing away in one corner with people sitting chatting away around their tables.

This was the place where the rich American businessmen would send their wives while they said they were away on business.

I had been tipped off by one of my mates about this place. He said either go on your own or with just two of you and go smartly dressed.

He said the American woman love the Guards and like to mother you.

I told one of my friends about this. His name being Benny.

Benny was a Geordie lad worked out on the gym but still looked thin. He had dark hair a huge smile but looked like he had not left school long.

We had been out quite a lot together him to my house and me up to Newcastle.

We both got into a few fisticuffs here and there.

Well this night we shit, showered, and shaved. Put on our suits and went of downtown. We popped in a few locals where the other lads were and had a few drinks with them until about ten o'clock and then headed to Café de Paris.

The doorman let us in after giving us the once over and we walked down the stairs and into the club.

It was not very packed at this time, so we ordered some drinks and took a seat.

There were a few women in, but none took our fancy even though we said we would grab a granny if it came to it.

About an hour past and the place filled up a bit. A group of women sat on a table next to us and started having a bit of a laugh with us and before you knew it, we were dancing with each of them laughing around and letting them enjoy us.

The women were all British, but we had a good laugh with them before they left.

We were then on our own again and the place was now packed.

We had both come to the conclusion that we would not be pulling tonight. But then a woman who was in her mid-40s approached me. She was well dressed in a skintight dress on and a reasonable figure.

She said why hello would you mind if my partner and I join you.

I said no come over and join us. Her friend was also in her 40s but a little bit older.

They sat down and said you two seemed to be enjoying yourselves.

I said yeah, they were a great bunch of ladies.

We then got talking about one thing and another mainly us asking them questions and me interpreting for Benny as they could not understand even one word he was saying.

Benny asked the ladies if they wanted a drink, I interpreted, and he then went over and got them.

The ladies then asked us how old we were, so we added a few years on, but they still thought we were a lot younger.

Then it was the masterstroke. I said we have both been in the army for six years so we cannot be as young as you have said.

You both soldiers she said? Yes, we are both in the Coldstream Guards, I said.

No not the ones who stand outside the Queen's house with the busbies on, and the red jackets?

Yes, that's us we said.

The questions then started flying _ have you ever met the Queen? How are the two princes? Why can't you smile? Can we meet you in your uniform?

We answered the questions the best we could and then had a couple of drinks with the ladies before they asked us back to their apartments.

I went into my room with mine and with Benny his.

My Yank dame then told me to lie on the bed as she undressed and started kissing me from the toes all along my body stopping at several places.

She said she was going to teach me things that I have never done before and would properly never do again. (I will try anything once.)

We had oral sex and did it in most positions and when we had finished, she said I was not bad for a young lad and we would spend the day in bed tomorrow, which we did for the morning, and then Benny and I were treated by our sugar mummies to a shopping spree.

We arranged to meet them the next night and said we would see them for three days until their husbands returned from their convention wherever that was.

We did not turn up the next night and the two old American dames truly got fucked.

What we used to do for a lift back to the barracks was jump in a taxi where there were already some girls in, quickly chat them up and see which way the taxi was going.

If it were not going our way, we would jump out if the girls where not interested but if they were going our way, we would keep chatting them up until we neared Buckingham Palace. If they were nice we would go home with them if not then we would jump out, free taxi home.

One night, Benny and I had got ourselves into a fight down at the Punch and Judy in Covent Garden. We had given these three civvies a good kicking after they had minesweeped our beers and then given it the big one.

The police soon arrived, and we managed to get away but thought we would soon be caught so we jumped in a taxi, which had stopped at some traffic lights in Leicester Square. There were two girls in the taxi who straight away started complaining before we managed to talk them around.

They then said you're squaddies aren't you? Yea we said how you know. We are from St Thomas hospital they said. Nurses we asked, yea that is right they said, what regiment are you in?

We told the nurse what regiment we were in and then it was do you know him and him and him. Well, we knew all the lads the girls had mentioned but the girls had helped us out, so we went back with them and sneaked into their rooms.

We had a few drinks and started swapping spit with them.

Benny then went into the bathroom. I thought he must have been having a Richard the Third as he was in there for a while. But then he came out wearing a nurse's uniform and started doing a strip for us revealing bra, suspenders, stockings, and knickers. We were all in stiches laughing.

I was then asked to join in with the fancy dress, so I got dressed up the same.

We messed around a bit and then ran down the corridors shouting doctor, doctor.

We came to a fire exit with a green outside lit up. So, we opened the doors and ran out stripping of and shouting outside. Onto the small grass area, whereupon the security lights came on.

Windows opened nurses shouting at us; some laughing but others rather pissed off as we had just woken them as they were on shifts.

We soon had enough so went back over to the fire exit, but our girls shut the doors locking us out.

The next thing we knew four police officers came running over to us, along with security and grabbed us.

Two women two men police officers and two male security. At first, they thought we had broken in but our nurses then came to our aid like Florence Nightingale and told the police that we were there boyfriends. The police found out we were squaddies and let us of but warned all four of us that nurses had just finished shifts and we should all know better.

We went back to the rooms locked the doors and lay silent as we heard the security trying to find out where we were.

When it all was quite again, we had sex with the nurses and left early that next morning but we were in our clothes.

CHAPTER 11

Disasters

There have been many disasters in the army, whether it is your company being wiped out in a battle or your best friend shot. But these are the disasters for soldiers.

Squaddies disasters are when your wife runs off with your best mate or she is shagging it around. Worse still is if someone pinches your beer.

I had a three-day run of disasters starting with a seven-car pile-up on the M1.

I was travelling to Leeds along with three lads on a long weekend's leave.

Orville was one of the lads and he lived in Leeds, so we were going to watch Leeds United play football and go out and get ourselves pissed.

We were travelling up the M1 and had just past Woodall services and then 'bang' I had a blowout. The car (a horrible yellow/orange Allegro) started to spin and the next couple of minutes seemed to drag. My whole life quickly swept through my mind as I saw the central reservation coming straight at me. I had one of the lads just screaming another shouting my name and asking what I was doing and then there was Orville shouting, "We are all going to die," "We are all going to die."

I could see myself going straight through the barriers onto the oncoming traffic and rolling down the opposite bank, but someone was looking down on us as we hit the barrier and the car span around, stopping with the boot facing the traffic on our side.

I just remember thinking stay calm, stay calm as the car stopped.

The lads in the back seats were trying to get out the car but the child locks were on.

Everyone got out of the car unscratched. I sent the one with a dark jacket off down the motorway to flag down the traffic. Try and warn the oncoming traffic.

I then sent the lad with the white jacket off to telephone the police.

It once again seemed forever for the police to arrive and while we were waiting all hell broke out.

Cars only seeing my car at the last moment and swerving away. Then a Robin Reliant came and did not see my car and 'bang' it hit my car once again spinning my car around, taking my boot off and then it started turning over and rolling along the motorway. What a Robin Reliant was doing in the overtaking/fast last was beyond me.

We ran over to the car when it had stopped and pulled the door off. We then pulled the old chap out of the wreck. He was covered in blood and still holding his steering wheel which had sheared off.

I placed the old chap on my spare wheel that we had found and was hoping the police would soon turn up as the part of the motorway we were on was in darkness.

Then another car came; my car had been spun around so my headlights were now pointing at the oncoming traffic.

My car was in the fast lane, the Robin in the middle line about 50 metres further down the motorway.

A car came along saw mine, swerved and missed it. You could see the man thinking that was lucky then looked forward and there was the Robin. 'Bang' – another car joined us, and then it was another and another and then a lorry.

In all we were told there were about seven vehicles involved.

The police arrived, set up the lights and slowed the traffic. The traffic was now only using the hard shoulder and as I was sat in my written-off car with a policeman taking a statement, I could see the lads walking around picking up all our kit.

"Whose is this boot?" "Whose are these trousers?" And then Orville gets out the camera and the lads start posing as they use up the film.

I had two blowouts (I prefer the jobs) but was told none of the blame was mine.

As they say, things come in threes, well the second thing to happen this weekend was when we eventually got to Leeds, Orville and I went out on the piss.

We went down to Orville's local, which was full of locals and must have been a popular place, there were groups of lads and groups of girls, the décor being modern. With a large horseshoe bar, brass fittings, small sitting areas and a main area to stand not far from the bar. Groups of lads who you could see were mates and this was their regular meet up, nice looking girls a lot not with any men but looking at all the men. we then had quite a few beers. The place was very busy, and it was hard to get past people to get to the bar or the toilets.

Orville then accidently burnt a lad standing next to him with his cigarette. He said sorry to the lad, as it was an accident.

At first the lad was ok about it; he was smaller than Orville with long dark hair, wearing a stripped blue shirt and jeans, but then he suddenly just turned around and smacked Orville as Orville was looking away.

Orville hit the floor but got up of his arse and asked the lad why had he done this?

The lad just mouthed off.

So, I said, "What's your problem mate? My mate said he was sorry." The lad then asked, "You want some as well?" I said yes come on then and we started fighting but I this time put him on his arse.

The manager then came running over and said we had to leave. I explained, "We did not start it, and the other lad should have to leave." Orville then said, "Come on let's just go."

The manager told us to follow him out, so we followed him out the rear door and into the lobby. I thought this was strange as we had not entered the pub this way, Then I saw a lad about 6ft3 and built like Rocky enter the room and 'smack' he hit Orville who once again went onto his arse. I then smacked this lad, who rocked on his feet but did not go down, so I followed this up with a couple more before reaching my aim and putting him on his arse.

The lobby then just filled up with lads and I soon ended up on my arse on the floor as I felt punch after punch coming to my head from all directions. Then it was a free for all, my head became a football, and everyone seemed to want to score the winner. Somehow, I managed to crawl out of the lobby and got outside leaving a trail of blood behind me, just like a snail. Nobody followed.

The first thing I thought, "Where's Orville? He's still inside, they will kill him." I looked around for a weapon, any weapon would do. As I search frantically for this weapon so that I could go back into the gladiator's arena, I heard my name being called out from across the road. However, I ignored this as I was still dazed and still searched around for a weapon so I could go back in and save my comrade. But again, I could hear my name being called from across the road. So, I looked across the road through my bleared vision, blood still dripping down my face onto my top and could just make out Orville waving me to him. I hobbled across the road to him, blood pouring down my face, the swelling already starting, holding my ribs, I could only see out of one eye now.

It was Orville, I asked Orville if he was ok, and he replied he was.

I looked him up and down with my good eye. He had not even received a scratch and there was me, I had a broken cheekbone and was blind in my left eye for four days.

Orville's family wanted me to get the police involved but I did not and said I would deal with the matter myself, something you always say after your pride has been hurt, but something that rarely happens.

The third thing to happen was when I returned home my mates took me out on the piss to try and cheer me up but we were involved in another road accident and got into some bother with five lads and I spent the night in the cells after being arrested along with my mates for criminal damage and assault.

The charges were dropped latter. (What a weekend.)

I was on gate duty one day and one of my mates was late for parade.

I'm not going to give him a name, but on this day he returned late and I informed him he was in the shit for being AWOL (absent without leave).

He then broke down in front of me and started getting very upset, so I took him into my office and asked him what the matter was.

He had got off with a bird the night before down the West End and had gone back to her hotel room with her. He had sex with her and then she tied him up. He thought a bit of bondage might be different.

It certainly was, as in walks a big black bloke who gives him one up the dirt box, takes all his money and leaves him there. The maid in the morning finds him there, calls for the manager who then releases him.

I did not tell anyone else but told him it would be best if he told his company sergeant major.

One of our sergeants had a big family disaster or it would have been if he knew what had happened, or it got out what happened to his family.

He was in another company to the one I was in and was one of these sergeants who always wanted to be one of the lads.

He would go out on the piss with the lads whenever he could, making all kinds of excuses to his wife, so and so's birthday, so and so's leaving, so and so has been promoted, so and so has just returned from a posting and I haven't seen him for years, etc., etc.

He had two sons and two daughters. The daughters being about 15 the other 18.

The eldest daughter had been out with a few of the lads and really enjoyed sex.

One of the lads had been going out with a civvy girl for a while and on this night, they were having a party at her house.

All the lads were there and when the sergeant found out about it, he made his excuses and soon met up with the lads down the pub.

When they got to this house, the party was in full swing, with everybody now half pissed.

There was a lot of lads and a lot of girls at the house, some snogging in the kitchen, some in the garden and some in the lounge, others had gone upstairs.

The sergeant then noticed the lads coming and going from one of the bedrooms.

He asked what was happening and one of the new lads who did not really know the sarge told him that they were all taking it in turns on a right little goer in the room.

The sarge then had another can of beer and said he was not going to miss this.

Some of the lads told him not to go in the room, but the sarge had made his mind up, saying he was tired of the same old woman week in week out and wanted something fresh.

Another lad then walked out and the sarge walked into the dark room along with one of the lads, who quickly put his cock in the girl's mouth.

The sarge (always one of the lads) then took the girl from behind. Shot his load pretty quick before joining the rest of the lads, bragging how good he was and that he had lasted longer than anyone else and had taught her a thing or two.

The party went on all night and for some reason the girl in the room did not join the party and went off home.

The sarge would brag how good the party was for weeks later.

What he did not know and probably still does not is that the girl in the room was his daughter.

His daughter was told that her dad was downstairs and that is why she left. But she did not know that he was one of her many lovers of that night.

Another problem was whilst we were away on exercise or border patrol, our girlfriends and wives would be out on the town.

I was downtown on a few occasions, when I came back for rugby and was always getting chatted up by my comrade's wives, whilst they were earning the money for the bills.

However, I would never go with their wives, but that's me and other people did their own thing.

We caught a Yank climbing out of one of the lad's married quarters' windows.

We caught other lads from our battalion in hotels with someone else's wife.

But it is always the person who gets hurt who is the last to find out.

A friend of mine (not a friend at the time) did not know his wife was having an affair.

Everybody knew but not him, some lads tried to tell him, but he would go death to them.

His wife ran off with this lad every time he was away but was always, they're pretending that nothing had happened when he returned being the loving wife, she had missed him so much whilst he was away.

He gave her everything and she was never wanting. He treated her like his princess.

So, when it did finally sink in and he did start believing the lads, the shit hit the fan.

He had invited this bloke back to his house on several times, he thought this lad was a good mate, but all along this good mate was stabbing him in his back (along with stabbing his wife).

He went mad, the lads tried to calm him down, but he wasn't listening to any sense.

He went to meet his ex-mate to have it out with him.

He found his ex-best mate, who could tell straight away that he had been found out.

The ex-best mate then started to shit himself.

Starting at first with, "Don't believe the rumours, we are the best of mates," then seeing this wasn't working he started saying "Nothing went on," "Honest mate," "She tried it on, but I wouldn't do that to you," "It was only one kiss," "I won't see her again." Every word coming out of his mouth digging him deeper into the shit. The sweat pissing down his face, lie after lie coming from his gob and the odour coming from his trousers smelling like a pig farm.

Then the pig met the butcher as the knife was brought out and in it went, once, twice, three times.

Some of the lads watching then ran over and managed somehow to disarm the disarranged husband.

The pig survived and my friend was given free bed and breakfast for a couple of years at one of Her Majesty's establishments.

However, as they say, the butcher always gets his bacon, so if the pig reads this keep looking over your shoulder.

Jimmy, The Ginger Gigolo.

Jimmy would never have the problem of his wife messing around.

Why? you ask. Well, the answer to that is because he was only married for a day.

Jimmy was never lucky with women. He was skinner than Flat Stanley and his head glowed with his orange hair, he was pig ugly and loved his beer.

He met his woman of his dreams (probably his only ever woman).

He got his leg over and before you knew it, he was on Commanding Officer's orders asking permission to get married.

He got his permission, and the date was set up.

His mates told him to wait for a bit so he could get to know her, or more likely she could get to know him.

However, the big day was arranged.

His good lady along with her mum arranged the cake, flowers, dresses, bridesmaids, menu, disco, and anything else that needed arranging.

Jimmy arranged his stag night, his best man and his guard of honour all to be dressed in number ones. (Tunic and bearskin.)

The stag night went well, Jimmy got truly pissed and made a right twat of himself.

The big day then arrived. The mums had their best frocks on with blushing big hats, the grannies were there in there not so colourful dresses and drab hats.

The fathers were there trying to look smart in the suits that hide their aging beer bellies, the kids ran around like kids do with their mothers yelling at them to keep clean and then there was Jimmy and his guard of honour. Everyone wanting to look at these smart guardsmen with their red tunics, shining boots and combed bearskins.

Jimmy was feeling very proud and now and again he would put on his bearskin hiding his ginger mop and let people take photographs of him.

The service went well, Jimmy had a few beers beforehand to steady his nerves and was ok with his I DO.

After the service it was off to the reception, where upon the lads gave Jimmy a few more beers so he would be ready for the speeches.

The speeches went ok, but the people who knew Jimmy could see he was getting a little pissed.

Glasses of champagne then came, wine and more beer.

His new bride then had a little chat with him before the dancing started. Jimmy had then had just one too many as he turned to his new wife and told her to fuck off and leave him alone so he could enjoy himself with his mates. She ran off to her mother and started to sob her little heart out whilst Jimmy sunk a few more pints.

His father-in-law then approached him along with his new brother-in-law.

"What's going on? Why is my daughter crying? This is supposed to be the best day of her life."

"Fuck off will you, leave me alone, you don't understand me," replied Jimmy even more pissed now.

"Don't tell my dad to fuck off ginger bollocks," said the brother-in-law.

BANG, SMASH, WALLOP, CRASH.

Jimmy smacked his brother-in-law, Jimmy's father-in-law smacked Jimmy and all hell broke out.

The honour guard managed to stop the fight and calm Jimmy down taking him back to his room.

His best man then went to his bride, explaining that someone spiked his drink, and that Jimmy was sorry for all the trouble that he has caused.

The bride was having none of it and their first domestic was their last, no first dance, no leg-over on his wedding night and no honeymoon.

When the dust had settled, she still refused to see him, she filed for divorce and he hit the bottle and soon left the army.

CHAPTER 12

No Longer A Squaddie?

Before I finished in the army, I did a six months tour in Northern Ireland.

We were not allowed out on the piss, so there is not much to do for us true squaddies.

So, we just knuckled down and did some good soldiering.

West Belfast – fun and games, threatened, spat at, daily abuse, barracks blown up, shot at, riots all good fun.

A percentage of this book is going to combat stress. Whether it be the First or Second World War, Falklands, Bosnia, Gulf, Afghanistan or Northern Ireland whatever conflict there has been it has left armed forces personnel with PTSD.

There is a big problem when people leave the forces and find it hard to adjust to civilian life.

You might not have been in a conflict, but PTSD is a problem.

After this tour I then left the army. Thinking it was time to settle down. My father had also just died and brother had been involved in a hit and run and was in a wheelchair. So, I thought it was best to leave the army at this time.

No longer a squaddie? Well, I was honoured when one of my civvy mates said to me (after I was out of the army for a couple of years), "You're a true squaddie, you are still a fucking squaddie." He had been in the army, so I suppose he knows what he's talking about.

I got out of the army and went straight into a job. However, it was very difficult to adapt to civilian life.

Every night now my own, no more guard duty, barrack guard, exercises.

No more lads to go out with every night or talk to, no longer in this big family but now alone.

Some things where better, like I could go into the kitchen and help myself to food. A far cry from the times I spent in a trench starving and just dying for some food.

Nobody tells me what to do. I can wear what I liked, grow my hair, go where I wanted to.

No 0600hrs reveille, I could stay in bed. But I was alone, none of the comrades that I had strong bonds with, nobody to share the laughs and sadness.

I re-joined my old rugby club and met up with a lot of old mates. These were good mates but nothing like your squaddie mates.

I started going down the pubs with these lads. They worked on the door.

I worked on the door in London on several occasions.

This is when I started to see that Civvy Street was completely different from the army life when it came to fighting.

In the army if you got into a fight then everyone would be fighting.

In Civvy Street your army buddies were not there. So, there was a lot of one on one's.

In the army you could come home on leave and get into a fight, give someone a hiding and then return to your battalion.

In Civvy Street if you gave someone a good hiding and he came from a certain part of your town, then the next week you would be down the pub that bloke would be there and so would be his army of mates all tooled up. As I had been in the army for several years, I did not have that bond with my mates, I was just the lad who had left the army.

I ended up having a few fights when I first came out of the army and soon got a reputation for myself,

I had been told about one lad that you should not mess with with but when he came into the pub with his mates and started fighting with a mate, I got involved and ended up getting the better of him.

Another time I ended up fighting with an old ex-doorman who had a good reputation and again got the better of him and I then started to get a good reputation but these were one-on-one fights, nothing really like the army as I could feel that I did not have the backup like I used to.

My reputation must have been getting better as the police even left me alone one night when I had got into a fight with two carloads of lads.

These lads had started on a helpless young lad, and then went around a roundabout near to where me and my mate had just come out of the local pub. The car stopped and two lads got out and shouted, goaded and motioned to us to fight them, we went over smack, smack, they hit the floor and then the rest of the lads started getting out of the cars. The cars only had two doors so it became comical as they struggled to get out, we were knocking them down one by one.

We then could hear sirens and saw two police cars come screeching down the road, so we ran by the side of the pub and up a side street but then two police cars pulled up either side of us, blocking our escape, we had nowhere to run, my right hand covered in blood. To our surprise one of the windows went down and the police officer said, "Its ok it's just ____" my nickname and just drove off. The two carloads of lads had also made their escape.

I still do not know what police officers they were, but we were lucky.

On one occasion not long after getting out of the army I was down the local pub one night with my mates and all hell broke out.

My mate, a doorman for years, an ex-skinhead and top fighter in his time, got knuckle-dusted and his head was pouring with blood, the pub just went off with everyone fighting with a tough local gang.

The pub was a very lively pub, with the bar in the middle as you walked in, modern décor, tv screens around the walls, and different areas with seating. As you walked around the bar which was an oval shape you would come to the back doors leading into a big garden area. You would have different pubs being busy on different nights and groups would go from one pub to the other, so you would see the same faces. Rival gangs at each end of the pub.

My mate was short and stocky, balding quickly as each day passed, a five-inch by three-inch scar-come-skin-graft on his neck (this coming from a glass, in his skinhead days).

So on this evening it kicked off with this certain group,

We managed to get this group out of the pub after a long fight. Punches being received and given, glasses being thrown, a lot of screaming and shouting.

My mate then came over to me blood everywhere, we could see that this was a bad cut and he told us he had been knuckle-dusted and the lads had just gone out of the side door.

I then went into army mode as I told the lads to get tooled up and go and get them. There was a stash of saw off baseball bats kept by the front door on a shelf.

This is when I noticed the difference between army and civvy.

My army mates would have got tooled up and gone after these, but my civvy mates were worrying about the 'comeback'. This would be in days or weeks to come when this gang would get their team strength and come back down to the pub for revenge or even go around to your house.

My civvy mates were worried; they cannot go back to their battalion, whatever happened they had to face the consequences. They had families, girlfriends, houses, jobs, prison to think about. Usually, they would just leave it and put it down to another fight.

I once again said, "Come on lads get the baseball bats, let's get them."

This time it worked with a few of the doormen, two did not come, the adrenalin was still high, and we all got tooled up and ran up the road after this group and it was not long before we caught them. They turned and stood their ground, but they should have run as we got straight into them. My mate lashed out giving his knuckleduster mate four good smacks on the head with the baseball bat, they all hit the floor but somehow, they all managed to get away and off they ran across the busy road and into the distance.

We waited days then weeks and then months but there was no comeback from these lads, however this was the only time that we stood together like this and went after the fight.

I started doing the doors and did them for some ten years after. There have been many encounters with gangs and on most occasions the comeback happened.

I also got into trouble from time to time and ended up in court for GBH when a lad attacked me, and I hit him with one punch but took his lip off. I was found not guilty.

Other things in civvy life was like army life.

I went to a strip show on one night at the rugby club.

The two strippers were pretty rough.

There were about 50 blokes in the club, knocking down their favourite ales.

The club not being very big and was upstairs above the changing rooms. A small bar and seating area near to the pool table, an area for food.

One poor bloke was pulled up onto the floor and stripped by the strippers.

He was soon tossed away by the girls with the rest of us all laughing at the poor show that he had just put on.

The girls then went around the room trying to get someone else onto the floor.

One of the older fellows had been drinking for most of the day and had fallen asleep (the girls were that good). One of the girls then picked up a cane and whacked him with it several times. This soon woke him up. The girls tried to drag him up, but he was having none of it and just fell asleep again.

The girls then moved for me and being game for a laugh I joined them.

I was then stripped. I'm glad I was pissed as I was sitting there naked in front of all these blokes.

The girls then made me suck their tits and then gave me a Thomas the Tank.

I was then asked to lie down as one started sucking my manhood.

Then one got on top of me and started to pretend that she was fucking me.

She then whispered into my ear as I could hear all the lads telling me to give her one, "Pretend you are fucking me." I said, "I'm not pretending, you want to fuck me then jump on." She did not and kept rubbing her muff up and down along my shaft.

I then started to get a hard on and before you knew it, she punched me in the bollocks.

No more hard on, just aching balls and watery eyes.

Next thing I knew she sat on my mush and started with the old 69. I could hear the lads laughing their heads off, so as she was sat there, I held up my finger and got the response I wanted. "Give her it," "Shove it up her."

I then, to her shock, shoved my finger up her brown eye. She gave a yelp and jumped off as my mate tipped beer over her and sucked my finger clean (dirty bastard, throwing beer over her).

The pissed-off stripper then picked up my clothes and tossed them over the floor, my money going everywhere.

So, there was me walking around bollock naked asking people to mind while I picked up money and clothes from under their tables.

The rugby club has never had a stripper since.

There was another time something happened similar.

I was in Bali on rugby tour. We had just got to this mega hotel. Welcomed by the staff with a drink and shown to our rooms.

The hotel was next to the beach, it had a sunken bar in the swimming pool, and rooms were great, massage parlour, bars and a night club.

We got there too late to go into the town, so all went down to the club.

There was a few Japs in there doing karaoke. We got ourselves a few drinks and had a few songs and the Japs loved it.

The keys to the club were on the bar, so I locked us all in.

I then noticed one of the lads in the corner taking his clothes off.

So, I went over to him and asked him what he was doing? "Sock dance" was the reply I got from this off-duty police officer on tour with us. "Sock dance what's that?" I said. "Just take your clothes off and I will show you," said off-duty policeman. "But I'm not wearing any socks," I said.

He then tossed me one of his as we both stripped.

We both then put arms around each other like the cancan, went onto the stage, naked except for the rugby socks that we had on dangling from our manhood's.

It went down brilliantly, everybody laughing their socks off, but not putting them on their manhood's, except for the Japs who were trying to get out of the club but were unable to because of my locked door.

Paying your way.

On one trip away, a couple of us lads visited the red-light district in the local town.

The whores were very rough, but this did not stop a couple of the lads bagging up and spending a few pounds banging away.

I however did not fancy any of these dirty bitches.

Having a blowjob though was a different matter. The lads all chipped in for one of the younger lads to get off with this whore, he was given the money but shit himself when he got to the door and turned and handed the money to me.

I took it thankfully and went and got myself a blowjob (bagged up first).

On one night we visited the red-light district just to do some window-shopping and one young lad said, "Why don't me and you pay to watch Paul have sex with that whore."

I said, "I'm not paying money to watch someone shag someone else." But I said for a laugh I would go in with them if Paul, a heavily built lad with balding hair could shag her while she gave me head. We all agreed to this, haggled the whore down to about 12 quid and entered her room. We had all had a few beers and could not stop laughing as Paul and I stripped off and the young lad Dave watched.

The whore took it in turns giving Paul and I head whilst Dave kept looking only until we looked up at him laughing and he then turned his head in embarrassment.

Paul then took the whore from behind as she filled her mouth with my cock, I then got bored and knew I was not going to cum, so I debagged and had a piss.

Dave and I then got caught trying to nick her k-y jelly and she kicked us both out staying in there with Paul.

Dave then said he was shy and wanted to go with a whore on his own. He asked if I would wait for him, to which I said I would.

I was waiting and could hear the swish of a belt and then the slap as it made contact to bare flesh. This went on for about eight times, three minutes. Another ten minutes passed, then out walked Dave. I said, "Did you hear that? Someone in there was getting a right good whipping." Dave laughed and whispered, "It was me, I got whipped, but don't tell anyone will you?"

The next day he would walk past the lads getting onto the coach and they all would smack his arse. He looked at me and said "You bastard" as everyone burst out laughing.

Back home I once again saw a bit of difference from army life and civvy life.

I had been working on the door at a nightclub and we had a bit of trouble with some Asian lads.

We ended up having a street fight with them; I had punched one and kicked another in his balls. We managed to give them a good slapping and I had broken one of the lad's noses and knocked another lad's testicles so far up that when he opened his mouth you could see strands of pubic hair coming from the back of his throat.

One thing that should not happen was for trouble to come to your home, however it sometimes did. (The comeback.)

There was an unwritten rule saying, "Deal with it down the pubs and clubs and not at the homes as it was not fair to get wives and kids involved."

However, there were still people who would come to your homes to terrorise you and your family.

This had not happened to me, but I had fought with a few who would do this, so my house became a bit of a fortress.

A seven-foot rear gate, carpet grippers running along the top of this and also the fence, there was also nails sticking out of the top of the gate.

There were several nail traps going down the path between my garage and the fence.

Razor wire in several other places along the fences and ankle height in traps in other places. There was a garden light.

In the kitchen there were sensors pointing at the rear door and windows, an axe at the back door, a pick axe handle in the rear bedroom and one at the front door, CS gas spray hidden near the front and rear doors, a hammer in the front box room and my Gurkha's kukri by my bed and a knuckleduster in my bedside drawer.

Anyway after we had had the fisticuffs with these Asians who had kicked it off in the nightclub, I got the word back that the club was going to be burnt down and I was going to be shot.

I thought they were going a bit over the top here; it was only a fist fight and I did not even headbutt anyone.

I did not let it bother me too much, I just thought they should join the queue of people who said they were going to get me.

I was then informed a couple of days later that two carloads of them had turned up at one of the pubs in town. They had a shotgun and a couple of machetes.

Again, I did not let this bother me. They knew where I worked, so it was no use trying to scare me by turning up at a pub that I did not even go to.

However, one night I lay in bed alone and the phone rings at 2330hrs. I could not be bothered to answer it. I thought it would properly be some bird that I had given my number to, so I pressed 1471. It came up "Caller has withheld number."

It then rang again at 0050hrs and again at 0100hrs. I answered these calls but just got a funny noise and I could hear movement in the background. Nobody wanted to talk so I just put the phone down.

My head then started working overtime, had my number got out to these Asians?

Did they know where I lived?

I then pulled out my knife and waited, thinking to myself, shall I get in touch with some of my old army mates and sort it? Shall I get in touch with the lads I work with on the doors? Shall I just go to them and confront them or wait in ambush for the main one? Slit his throat? Get a gun? Put my army training into action?

I lay there in wait for them to turn up.

No more telephone calls since the last one.

Every car that went past I waited and listened, had it slowed down? Stopped? Could I hear people?

I had been trained for waiting in ambush and was really ready for the fight, a little bit of me wanting it.

The first one that came through the door would lose his arm, the second would see this before getting CS gassed, they would see that I meant it and I wasn't going to go down without a fight. They would now start to shit themselves.

I would now be swinging my Gurkha's kukri at them trying to use my first victim as a shield and as cover from any shotgun, I would make as much noise as possible and hope the neighbours would call the police.

My dog was with me, but this was not a good thing as he is a big softy and I would be trying to protect him as well as myself.

I thought about going around to Nigel's and stopping there the night, but in the end, I thought "Fuck it they will get more than they bargained for and I was not going to be driven out of my home by anyone."

I once again thought about getting a gun, but I would have to take the consequences with it. I was no longer in the army; I was just a mad ex-squaddie.

If I had a gun, I would have to use it and not pretend. However, this was Civvy Street and not a war, if I used it then I would be looking at doing time.

It was now 0155hrs, no more calls, plenty of cars going past, I lay there on my bed, shorts and trainers on, my hand clasped around my Gurkha's kukri waiting in the dark.

The morning came and all was ok. However, I did not want to go through that again.

I sent a message to them saying I was ready and willing to meet them. If I heard any more threat, then I would go to them.

I heard nothing back from them until a couple of weeks later.

They said they did not want to fight me and to forget the whole thing.

I suppose it was my head just playing tricks on me and if nothing else they did give me one sleepless night.

THE FINAL CHAPTER

12 Years on

I started writing this book some 16 years ago and did not know how I was going to end the book.

Since writing the book there has been the Bosnian War, two Iraq wars and then Afghanistan.

I have a beautiful daughter now who will be turning 14 in 2016, and yes, I'm not with my daughter's mother and still single.

I have moved in to four different houses and it was whist tidying up the garage in my latest house that I opened a box and found a floppy disk with Soldier Soldier written on it. That is that book I wrote years ago I thought, everyone told me to get it published but I kept putting it off.

So off I took it to work, my business which is going well and growing. I gave the floppy disk to my admin assistant, who looked at it with astonishment, "What's that he said?" Again time had passed and there are no floppy disks, cds, dvds, cd roms, Blu-ray, all new since I started the book. However, I did manage to get a disk driver with a floppy disk drive and managed to install this to my laptop.

I then sat back before reading the book again and thought had my life changed much? Had I settled down??

The answer to that question is yes, I have now settled down in my life, no more nightclubs, no more pubs, but this has only happened in the last couple of months after what I call was my final scare, something that has made me sit back and look at my life.

I'm now a successful businessman and now a director of three companies. I have played and got paid for playing rugby union and then moved into coaching and coached rugby union at three of the local clubs, and have been successful in this, winning promotions, getting to cup finals, and winning the team of the year in the *Rugby World Magazine* which resulted in me being on the front cover.

It may have only been in the bottom right-hand corner but still on the front cover holding the cup with my right hand in plaster.

Why was my hand in plaster?

Well on rugby tour I again manage to get myself into a little scuffle.

I was coaching our team and after a successful long season which resulted in us winning promotion as champions and getting into the Warwickshire shield final, we all went off to Spain on tour.

I was walking along a street in Seoul with a friend of mine and a Spanish lad. The evening being warm after a hot day, across the road was a lad about 6ft tall, dark-skinned, smashing up shop windows and being very violent.

He approaches one of our rugby lads on the other side of the road. This lad was in his forties, had not played rugby but was on tour for the beer and women, he was staggering up the road wearing his pink swimming cap which was made to wear for falling into the hotel pool the previous night at 2am drunk, waking up other guests. So, he was made to wear this hat for 24 hours as punishment from the kangaroo court.

Well, the violent chap then started to verbally abuse our pinky. He then noticed me across the other side of the road and told the violent chap to see me.

And this is what happened. He approached me and told me he wanted to fight me. I thought about it but told the Spanish lad I was with to tell him in Spanish to leave as I was not interested in spending a night in a Spanish cell.

With this the violent chap walked in front of me and stood his ground. Raised his fists and told me he was the Moroccan boxing champion. I quickly threw a right-hand shot and put this champion onto the floor. At this time, I could see that my hand was not right. The champion then started to get up. I looked at my hand then turned to JP the lad I was with. JP being taller than me about 6ft2 and stocky. "You're going to have to do him for me JP," I said. But I could tell this was not going to happen. As the champ was getting to his feet, I then kneed him into his ribs sending him to the floor again before starting to tap dance on him. He did not get up and I became the new boxing champion of Morocco.

We then moved into a nightclub and I implanted my hand into a bucket of ice. After a couple of minutes, I pulled my hand out and notice something sticking out. I thought this was my knuckle being pushed out of place. So, I had a couple of shots. We had met up with James a young lad who was always in trouble, liked to strip off or walk around naked with only a pizza box to cover him with his small tool sticking out of a purpose-built hole.

James then held my arm and JP pushed the protruding object back in place. We then went on to have a few more beers before playing our tour match the next day. Bandaged hand, I stayed on the pitch for the first half but then withdrew myself. Not because of the hand but because of the 20 beers and 15 shots from the night before.

When I returned to England, I had the hand x-rayed and the doctor had said that it was not my knuckle but I had broken my bone and the person who had put it back in place had done a better job than the hospital would have done. So that why I'm on the front page of the *Rugby World Magazine* wearing a cast. I did tell JP that he should now look at changing careers into the medical sector.

Now back to my final scare and the thing that has now sorted me out.

At the time I had started my own business up training people in the construction industry whilst still working for the local government as an environment noise monitoring officer.

My neighbour who also used to work for the same unit and was my boss was having a stag night. We had decided that we would go out for a meal and a few drinks in a town near to us, so that we could enjoy ourselves not worrying about bumping into anyone whose stereo we might have taken.

There was going to be about seven of us on this night out. All working professionals. We had a local councillor with us, my manager and two managers from a different organisation and a couple of other lads, all in full-time employment.

We went to the restaurant and took our seats, the restaurant being a Gurkha's restaurant, so there were a lot of pictures of their homeland on the green walls and several sets of kukri on the walls.

Andy then was ushered into the toilet, where we made him put on his sumo costume. After a nice meal we moved onto several pubs before ending up at the nightclub.

The nightclub which was one of a chain of nightclubs throughout the UK was not very busy when we entered. The bar being central, with the toilets to the left and the dancefloor to the far end away from the door. There were several seating cubicles. A couple sitting in one and at the bar there was several girls. We moved over to theses who all wanted photograph with Andy in his sumo suit.

We then had a few beers and as the girls had taken to our group, we started dancing with them.

Soon the club started to fill up and it was not long before it was hard to move around without banging into someone.

It was getting near to midnight. Andy was drunk and really enjoying himself, like the rest of our group – Andy, being a happy drunk.

Then all hell broke out. I was standing near the toilets chatting to a girl when a lad came charging past me. He was quite thin with dark hair. He pushed past me knocking all my beer over my white shirt. I was soaked in beer. He then came over to me. "An apology would be nice," I said. "Fuck you," he said and walked off over to two other lads. These lads were in their mid-20s, tall and broad. Both being well over 6ft and both looking physical fit. No beer belly or grey balding hair, like I had now got.

I could see them pointing over to me. With the experience I had I knew this was a bad situation to be in. The lads I was out with were not fighters they were just working men on a good night out. I had no army mates with me or doormen.

Things then happened very quickly. One of the lads started speaking to me as the others came around me.

"What's your problem mate?" he said. "I only asked your mate for an apology, look, it was only a drink, it will come out in the wash don't worry about it mate," I said. "Why should he apologise to you, you fat fucker?" he replied.

I looked around and none of the lads I was with could be seen. I then felt a hand around my head and looked up as this lad pulled me towards him, whispering in my ear, "Who do you think you are? You're going to get it, you fat fucker. You ain't leaving here alive tonight."

At this time, I really feared for the worst. I was away from my hometown where most people and doormen knew me, the lads I was out with were not the fighting type. I had got older and now carrying a few extra pounds and these lads were young and fit, you could tell that they were not scared and had been involved in violence before. The old days of a fisticuffs had gone, had they got any weapons on them? This was all going through my head. I then noticed him put his drink down and turned towards me. But my past had not left me, there was still fight in this old dog. As he approached me, I pulled back my head, something that I had done on many occasions and then unleashed the hammer blow of my head. I could hear and feel the contact as my head smashed against his. He fell to the floor. I then looked out to my right and could see his mate shouting and charging at me throwing punches. I unleashed a left and then a right as he fell to the floor at the same time, I felt a bang on my head. It was a bottle. I turned and again lashed out bodies flying everywhere. I did not know who was attacking me, but I was fighting for my life. Blood pouring down my bald head. I could then see the second lad getting off the floor and I made sure that he would no longer be a problem to me.

With this, the lads I was out with got involved pushing people away from me and trying to stem the situation.

The police soon arrived, and I spent the night in the cells again. I was released on bail, but the case went onto crown court with me being charged for ABH and Affray, all on CCTV. The two lads had pressed charges against me, both the big young fighting machines, who were nursing a broken cheekbone, stitches above the eye, knocked-out teeth, stamp marks – and damaged pride that they had been beaten by an old, fat, bold chap.

The case went to the Magistrate's Court who in turn passed it over to crown court and the case carried on for over a year. I stopped going out thinking that every time I went out, I would end up in trouble somebody starting on me. I had to take redundancy from my job with the council as I was told that if found guilty then I would be sacked.

The whole process took it out of me. I was not scared of going to prison, it might do me good. Lose a bit of weight. But who was going to look after my two British bulldogs, how was I going to pay my mortgage, and most of all I would miss out on seeing my daughter?

So, after many years of many misadventures I am glad to say that hopefully I have grown up and settled down a bit. I would rather stay in and watch the soaps. Leave the night life to the younger ones.

PS. I was found not guilty on two charges.

I hope this book has not offended anyone and has been a good read.

I am now 54 with my daughter being 18. This is the time to finally get the book published after over 25 years of it sat around, and hopefully there will not be a Part 2.

Nulli Secundus.

www.ingramcontent.com/pod-product-compliance
Lightning Source LLC
Chambersburg PA
CBHW030105070426
42448CB00037B/969